WALKING
PARIS

WALKING

PARIS

THE BEST OF THE CITY

Pas Paschali
Brian Robinson

NATIONAL GEOGRAPHIC
Washington, D.C.

WALKING
PARIS

CONTENTS

PART 1

PAGE 12
WHIRLWIND TOURS

PART 2

PAGE 36
PARIS'S NEIGHBORHOODS

PART 3

PAGE 174
TRAVEL ESSENTIALS

Cathédrale de Notre-Dame de Paris (previous pages); rue de Rivoli (left); Notre-Dame (top right); "Venus de Milo" in the Musée du Louvre (right)

Introduction

I'm walking down the rue du Bac in the Paris neighborhood of St.-Germain-des-Prés. I'll reach the end of the street and simply, aimlessly choose a direction to walk. I don't have anywhere in particular that I must go. Eventually, I'll get to the museums and galleries and other places I've told myself I'll visit. While Paris is erecting great structures of modernity, its real charm lies in the small, the intimate, the old. Which is why I'm compelled to wander, to get as close as possible to the city's *itness*. I might linger in the Jardin des Tuileries (and if I do, I will inevitably end up at the Musée de l'Orangerie, home to Monet's seductive "Water Lilies"). And I will almost certainly linger in a café that serendipitously catches my fancy.

Paris is perhaps the world's most lustrously cinematic city. The streets seem like film sets populated by charming eccentrics, drop-dead gorgeous fashionistas, professorial types, beyond cute kids. And, while all of these can be found in other cities, add the

No. 29 avenue Rapp, near the Tour Eiffel, was designed by Jules Lavirotte and completed in 1901.

Parisian *soupçon*—dogs, thousands of them, in every shape and size—and you have a streetscape unlike any other. I do have my favorite places. Some are conventional landmarks—the Louvre, Musée d'Orsay—but many are not. More obscure treasures include the Peace Garden at UNESCO's world headquarters and the Musée du Vin in the former cellars of the Passy Abbey. And while I love to wander a city aimlessly, you may want to take more purposeful walks. This guide will be indispensable.

Keith Bellows
Editor in Chief, National Geographic Traveler *magazine*

Visiting Paris

Of all world capitals, Paris is the most chic. Its attractive mélange of haute couture and top-end cuisine, spectacular art collections and architectural spectacle, Gothic churches and romantic cafés, makes it—justifiably—the most visited city in the world.

Paris in a Nutshell

The Seine River divides the city into the Right Bank (Rive Droite) and Left Bank (Rive Gauche), with two islands—Île de la Cité and Île St.-Louis—sitting between. The first settlers, a Celtic tribe called the Parisii, inhabited the Île de la Cité in the third century B.C. Around 500 years later, the city was christianized and the first churches were built. The Middle Ages saw the building of the Cathédrale de Notre-Dame de Paris and a fortress that became the Palais du Louvre.

In the 17th century, the Jardin des Tuileries and Jardin du Luxembourg were built for royal pleasure, and King Louis XIV moved the royal court from the Louvre to Versailles. In the 19th-century, Napoleon I built his monumental arches and, under Napoleon III, Baron Haussmann

Paris Day-by-Day

Open every day (with some exceptions for major public holidays) Arc de Triomphe, Musée du Cinéma, La Conciergerie, Les Invalides, Musée Jacquemart-André, Musée du Luxembourg, Notre-Dame, Panthéon, Pinacothèque de Paris, Sacré-Coeur, Ste.-Chapelle, Tour Eiffel. The Musée Picasso is closed until Spring 2013.

Monday Many museums are closed except for the above and Centre Pompidou, Grand Palais, Musée d'Art et d'Histoire du Judaïsme, Musée de Cluny, Musée de l'Orangerie. Musée du Luxembourg is open until 11 p.m.

Tuesday National museums are closed. Fondation Cartier is open until 10 p.m.

Wednesday Grand Palais and Musée du Louvre are open until 10 p.m.

Thursday Musée d'Art Moderne is open until 10 p.m.; Musée des Arts Décoratifs until 9 p.m.; Musée d'Orsay until 9:45 p.m.; Musée du Quai Branly until 9:30 p.m.

Friday Musée du Louvre is open until 10 p.m.; Musée du Luxembourg until 10 p.m.; Musée du Quai Branly until 9:30 p.m.

Saturday Musée d'Art et d'Histoire du Judaïsme is closed. Musée du Luxembourg is open until 10 p.m.; Musée du Quai Branly until 9:30 p.m.

Sunday Most museums and attractions are open on Sunday. National museums are free on the first Sunday of the month.

Paris cafés stay open late, with people sipping drinks until well into the night.

replaced the city's maze of medieval streets with grand boulevards.

Navigating Paris

The city is divided into 20 districts (arrondissements), starting with the first arrondissement in the center and working outward in a spiral. Most maps of Paris chart the city by arrondissement and give each street's arrondissement in the street index.

Enjoying Paris for Less

If you've arrived from London by Eurostar, your ticket grants you two-for-one admission at any of the national museums, including the Louvre. Most art galleries are free and hold *vernissages* (private viewings) on Thursday or Friday evenings, when you may even be offered a free glass of wine. Notre-Dame offers early-evening recitals, but for a comprehensive guide to free concerts buy a copy of *Pariscope* magazine. For a month from mid-July, the Seine's banks are converted into *plages* (beaches), complete with live music and other amusements. One weekend in October, *Nuits Blanches* (literally White Nights, meaning an all-nighter) offer dusk-till-dawn arts events in buildings around the city.

Using This Guide

The tours in this guide explore Paris's most interesting corners. Each tour is plotted on a map and has been planned to fill a day, taking into account opening hours and the times of day when sites are less crowded. Many end near restaurants, theaters, or lively night spots for evening activities.

USING THIS GUIDE

Whirlwind Tours

Whirlwind Tours are for people who have only a day or a weekend to spend in the city and want to be sure that they see the best of the best. Choose your tour based on your time and interests: One Day; Weekend (Day 1 & Day 2); For Fun; and With Kids (Day 1 & Day 2).

Tips For the Day and Weekend Tours, a Tips spread following the itinerary map provides insider information on detours from the key sites, extra places to see, nearby cafés and restaurants, and ideas for adapting the tours to suit your interests.

Site Descriptions

In the For Fun and With Kids tours, key sites spreads following the maps provide descriptions of all the sites and practical information for visitors.

Neighborhood Tours

The nine neighborhood tours each begin with an introduction, followed by an itinerary map highlighting the key sites that make up the tour and detailed key sites descriptions. Each tour is followed by an "in-depth" spread showcasing one major site along the route, a "distinctly" Paris spread providing background information on a quintessential element of that neighborhood, and a "best of" spread that groups sites thematically.

Itinerary Map A map of the neighborhood shows the locations of the key sites, métro stations, and main streets.

Captions These blurbs briefly describe the key sites and give instructions on finding the next site on the tour. Page references direct you to full descriptions of the sites on the following pages.

Route Dotted lines link the key sites.

Price Ranges for Key Sites

€	€1–€5
€€	€6–€10
€€€	€11–€15
€€€€	€16–€20
€€€€€	over €20

Price Ranges for Good Eats (for one person, excluding drinks)

€	under €25
€€	€25–€40
€€€	€40–€60
€€€€	€60–€90
€€€€€	over €90

Key Sites Descriptions These spreads provide a detailed description and highlights for each site, following the order on the map, plus each one's address, website, phone number, entrance fee, days closed, and nearest métro station.

Good Eats Refer to these lists for a selection of cafés and restaurants along the route.

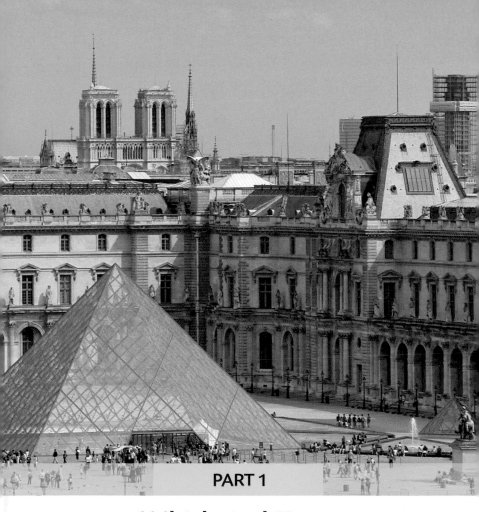

PART 1

Whirlwind Tours

Paris in a Day

See the best of the city on this packed one-day tour.

⑤ Jardin des Tuileries and Avenue des Champs-Élysées (see pp. 78, 118–119, 131) The Tuileries Garden is perfect for a rest before a stroll up France's grandest avenue. Cross the busy Place de la Concorde to the eastern end of the Champs-Élysées.

⑥ Arc de Triomphe (see pp. 138–139) Situated at the meeting of 12 roads, Napoleon's massive victory arch is adorned with some of the city's best sculpture. From beneath the arch, take the métro three stops to Trocadéro station and cross the river.

⑦ Tour Eiffel (see p. 149) Cap off the day by ascending to the iron giant's second level, for a spectacular view across the entire city.

PARIS IN A DAY   DISTANCE: 4.8 MILES (7.7 KM)
TIME: APPROX. 9 HOURS   MÉTRO START: CITÉ

WHIRLWIND TOURS

4 Musée du Louvre
(see pp. 122–125) **Skip the crowds around the "Mona Lisa" and head to "Winged Victory," one of antiquity's greatest sculptures (Escalier Deru, Ground Floor, Denon Wing). Head west, past the Arc de Triomphe du Carrousel toward the formal gardens.**

3 Boulevard St.-Germain
(see pp. 16–17, 26) **Make like Pablo Picasso, Jean-Paul Sartre, and Simone de Beauvoir and dine at one of the trio of celebrated cafés along the Left Bank's moody boulevard—Brasserie Lipp, Café de Flore, or Les Deux Magots. Follow rue Bonaparte and Quai Malaquais, then cross Pont du Carrousel to the north side of the Seine River.**

1 Cathédrale de Notre-Dame de Paris
(see pp. 48–49) **Both a religious mecca and cultural icon, this Gothic cathedral looms above the Île de la Cité and the Seine River. From the square in front of Notre-Dame, cross the Petit Pont bridge and move down rue St.-Jacques to rue du Sommerard.**

2 Musée de Cluny (see pp. 64–65) **This museum of the Middle Ages is home to some of the world's finest medieval art. The Roman baths are also worth a look. Head west out of the museum, and then take a right onto boulevard St.-Michel.**

Tips

Few cities have so many world-class museums, majestic monuments, and beautiful gardens packed into such a compact area, which makes Paris ideal for anyone with only a day to spare. Yet if time is short, you may wish to customize your time with these excellent, and less crowded, alternatives.

❶ **Cathédrale de Notre-Dame de Paris** (see pp. 48–49) If you're content with gazing at Notre-Dame's fine Gothic architecture from the outside only, spend some time exploring the Île de la Cité instead. Stroll around the ■ ANCIEN CLOÎTRE QUARTIER (see p. 46), a warren of old streets north of the cathedral, to imagine the island during

Today, you're more likely to find tourists than philosophers at Les Deux Magots.

its medieval heyday. The ■ MARCHÉ AUX FLEURS (see pp. 45–46), a fabulous and fragrant year-round flower market, makes a colorful excursion. On Sundays, some of the flower stalls make way for the sale of caged birds.

❷ **Musée de Cluny** (see pp. 64–65) After exploring this medieval museum, and if you like your history on the dark side, check out the nearby ■ MUSÉE DE LA PRÉFECTURE DE LA POLICE *(4 rue de la Montagne Ste.-Geneviève, 5th arr., 01 44 41 52 50, closed Sun. and public holidays),* with its displays on the city's criminality and police force from medieval times to today, including a display of weaponry and a revolution-era guillotine.

❸ **Boulevard St.-Germain** If lunch at one of boulevard St.-Germain's legendary cafés, such as Les Deux Magots (see p. 158) and Café de Flore (see p. 158), doesn't take your fancy, try ■ RUE DE BUCI (*6th arr.*) instead. This foodie street offers a good range of fruit and vegetable stalls, brasseries, cafés, and restaurants from which to choose.

❹ Musée du Louvre (see pp. 122–125) This palace rivals all other Paris buildings in beauty. If you can't face the crowds (or the lines to get in), it's still worth wandering around the outside of the building to enjoy its elegant exterior. Look for mid-17th-century architect Claude Perrault's ■ COLONNADE on the easternmost facade, whose columns are a masterpiece of baroque architecture.

❺ Jardin des Tuileries and Avenue des Champs-Élysées (see pp. 118–119, 131) If you're walking through the Tuileries Garden during summer, make some time to enjoy the ■ FÊTE DE FORAINE (*www.feteforaine -jardindestuileries.com, 06 63 70 28 22, open July–Aug.*). Its 60 or more fairground attractions include a merry-go-round, bumper cars, and a Ferris wheel that gives great views of the Louvre. Walk up the ■ CHAMPS-ÉLYSÉES, which has broad sidewalks shaded by trees and lined with cafés, restaurants, car showrooms, and other stores. If you want to avoid the crowds, head a little farther north to the peaceful ■ JARDIN DES CHAMPS-ÉLYSÉES, which has many statues, fountains, flowers, and benches.

CUSTOMIZING **YOUR DAY**

After your day's tour, take in some of Paris's celebrated nightlife. Immortalized by artists such as Henri de Toulouse-Lautrec, the **Moulin Rouge** (see p. 171) nightclub continues to sizzle after 120 years in show biz. Check out *www.timeout.com/Paris* or *www.gogo paris.com* for reviews and listings of clubs, bars, and theaters.

❻ Arc de Triomphe (see pp. 138–139) Contemporary art enthusiasts can walk down avenue d'Iéna to the ■ PALAIS DE TOKYO (*13 ave. du Président Wilson, 16th arr., www.palaisdetokyo .com, 01 47 23 51 01, €€, closed Mon.*), a vast art deco building that hosts shows of sculpture and installation art.

❼ Tour Eiffel (see p. 149) There is no alternative to this Parisian symbol nearby, but you can beat the lines by booking tickets in advance (*www .eiffel-tower.com*). Ride the elevator to the tower's second level to savor one of the globe's most tantalizing views. If you wish only to look up at the tower from the ground, use the time you save to head to ■ AVENUE RAPP, less than 0.6 mile (1 km) to the east of the tower. The doorway of No. 29, designed by architect Jules Lavirotte in 1901, is decorated in art nouveau style.

DAY
1

Paris in a Weekend

The Rive Droite (Right Bank) is the focus of the first day of your Parisian adventure, from the stately Louvre to artsy Montmartre.

BOULEVARD DES BATIGNOLLES

AVE DE CLICHY

AVE DE ST-OUEN

RUE DE CLICHY

RUE D'AMSTERDAM

⑤ Place du Tertre and Montmartre's Streets (see pp. 164–166) Get your portrait done at Place du Tertre or wander around this artsy hilltop hangout.

Musée Cernuschi

Gare St.-Lazare

RUE DU HAVRE

St.-Augustin

RUE DE LA PÉPINIÈRE

BOULEVARD HAUSSMANN

RUE TRONCHET

BLVD. DES

PLACE VENDÔME

RUE

JARDIN DES TUILERIES

❶ Musée du Louvre (see pp. 122–125) Not only can you explore this Renaissance palace, but you can also see the remains of the medieval castle it was built on. Head east along the river and cross over on Pont Notre-Dame.

Musée d'Orsay

QUAI

RUE DU BAC

PARIS IN A WEEKEND DAY 1   DISTANCE: 4 MILES (6.4 KM)
TIME: APPROX. 9 HOURS   MÉTRO START: PALAIS-ROYAL MUSÉE DU LOUVRE

18 | WALKING PARIS

❹ Basilique du Sacré-Coeur (see pp. 168–169) The terraces in front of the basilica offer one of Paris's most spectacular views. If you wish, ascend the church's teardrop-shaped dome for an even higher vantage point. Head west along parvis du Sacré-Coeur toward rue du Cardinal Guibert and the warren of streets that comprise Montmartre.

❸ Centre Pompidou (see pp. 90–91) The Pompidou Center's colorful exterior rises above the Right Bank's ancient mansions. Walk west along rue Rambuteau to Les Halles station, take the M4 métro (direction Clignancourt) to Barbès Rochechouart, walk west to the base of the hill and take the funicular railway.

❷ Cathédrale de Notre-Dame de Paris (see pp. 48–49) Paris's medieval cathedral was fully refurbished in the 19th century following centuries of neglect and, during the revolution, destruction. Retrace your steps across the Pont Notre-Dame and head north along rue St.-Martin.

DAY
2

Paris in a Weekend

Paradigms of 19th-century Paris—Impressionist art, the Arc de Triomphe, the Tour Eiffel, and café society—highlight your weekend's second day.

❹ Bateau Mouche Cruise
(see p. 23) **Catch a boat along the Seine River, boarding from between the Invalides and Alma Bridges. Cruises last about 1.25 hours. After disembarking, head east along the river, then north up avenue Franklin D. Roosevelt.**

❺ Avenue des Champs-Élysées
(see p. 131) **Take an early evening stroll heading west along France's most famous thoroughfare, window shopping along the way and taking in the tree-lined avenue's electric atmosphere.**

❻ Arc de Triomphe (see pp. 138–139) **Make your way to the roof of Napoleon's massive arch for a look across a Parisian evening. Take the métro from Charles de Gaulle Étoile to Trocadéro, walk through the gardens and across Pont d'Iéna.**

❼ Tour Eiffel (see p. 149) **Ascend to the highest level for a grand look across the city at night or admire Paris's tallest tower from the ground. The tower is open until 11 p.m. (midnight in summer).**

Musée
Jacquemart-
André

La Défense
Arc de Triomphe ❻ Ⓜ Charles de
Gaulle Étoile
Lido

AVE. DE FRIEDLAND

AVENUE FOCH
AVENUE

Avenue des
Champs-Élysées

Palais de
l'Élysée

Office du
Tourisme ❺

DES CHAMPS-ÉLYSÉES

AVENUE D'IÉNA

AVENUE VICTOR HUGO

AVENUE D'IÉNA

AVENUE MARCEAU

Franklin D.
Roosevelt Grand
Palais

Bois de
Boulogne

Palais
de Tokyo

COURS
ALBERT 1er

Petit
Palais

P. DES INVALIDES

Ⓜ Trocadéro

AVE. DE NEW YORK

Seine ❹

Bateau
Mouche Cruise

PONT DE L'ALMA

Palais de
Chaillot
JARDINS
DU
TROCADÉRO

PONT D'IÉNA

Musée du
Quai Branly

QUAI D'ORSAY Ⓜ Invalides

ESPLANADE
DES INVALIDES

QUAI BRANLY

❼ Tour Eiffel

AVENUE BOSQUET

BLVD. DE TOUR MAUBOURG

Les
Invalides

PARC DU
CHAMP
DE MARS

LA MOTTE-PICQUET

AVE. DE TOURVILLE

Musée
Rodin

RUE DE

RUE DE BRETEUIL

École
Militaire

AVE. DE LOWENDAL

BLVD. DES INVALIDES

BOULEVARD DE GRENELLE

BLVD. GARIBALDI

UNESCO

AVE. DE SUFFREN

BLVD. PASTEUR

BLVD. DE

Gare
Montparnasse

0   1 mile
0   1 kilometer

WHIRLWIND TOURS

❸ Musée d'Orsay (see pp. 154–155)
It's hard to decide what is more
spectacular, the restored beaux arts
railway station or the 19th-century
art within. Head west on Quai Anatole
France, following the river to Pont de
l'Alma, then cross to the north bank.

❷ Boulevard St.-Germain (see
pp. 16–17, 26) Once frequented by
existentialists, the area is now known
for its plush shops and art galleries.
Turn right on rue du Bac, then head
west along Quai Anatole France and
the Seine River.

❶ Musée de Cluny (see pp. 64–65)
Check out some of the world's finest
15th-century tapestries, such as
"The Lady and the Unicorn," in
Room 13. Turn west on boulevard du
Sommerard and then turn right onto
boulevard St.-Michel.

Tips

Two days in the French capital affords enough time to see all of the city's main sites, including plenty of world-class art and architecture, as well as a few impressive smaller attractions. Use these tips to customize your weekend, and watch for some of the lesser-known sites along your way.

DAY 1

❶ **Musée du Louvre** (see pp. 122–125) If the Louvre is too daunting for you, visit the ■ MUSÉE DE L'ORANGERIE (see pp. 119–120), which displays its art, including Monet's paintings of water lilies, in an intimate atmosphere.

❷ **Cathédrale de Notre-Dame de Paris** (see pp. 48–49) Before you enter the city's famous medieval cathedral,

Square du Jean XXIII is a good place to relax.

take time to admire the 19th-century equine ■ STATUE OF CHARLEMAGNE, king of the Franks in the eighth century, out front. Also look for ■ POINT ZERO, Paris's official center and the point from which all roads leading to the capital are measured. For some peace and reflection, head to the back of the cathedral to the ■ SQUARE DU JEAN XXIII, which has plenty of benches shaded by lime, elm, and cherry trees.

❸ **Centre Pompidou** (see pp. 90–91) Before ascending the escalators to the ■ MUSÉE NATIONAL D'ART MODERNE, set aside an hour for lunch at one of the eateries around the cobblestone piazza. ■ RESTAURANT DAME TARTINE (*2 rue Brisemiche, 4th arr., 01 42 77 32 22*) tenders outdoor tables with a menu of French classics like *croque monsieur, tartines* (open-faced sandwiches), salads, crepes, and desserts. Its tables overlook the ■ Stravinsky Fountain, 16 pieces of water-based sculpture inspired by the composer's work. On the plaza's other side, ■ Riad Nejma (*141 rue St.-Martin, 4th arr., www.riadnejma.com, 01 42 78 35 00*) serves Moroccan cuisine.

❺ Place du Tertre and Montmartre's Streets (see pp. 164–166) If you're a fan of Salvador Dalí, visit the ■ Espace Dalí Montmartre (*11 rue Poulbot, 18th arr., www.daliparis.com, 01 42 64 40 10, €€*), a permanent collection of 330 dramatically lit works from the surrealist painter, along with Dalí's recorded voice playing in the gallery.

DAY 2

❷ Boulevard St.-Germain Although St.-Germain is well known for its existential philosophy, for a more materialist experience, visit the ■ Musée de la Monnaie (*11 quai de Conti, 6th arr., 01 40 46 56 66, closed Mon., €€*), the former state mint. Here you can find out about French coinage from 300 B.C.—when money first appeared in Gaul—right up to the modern day.

❸ Musée d'Orsay (see pp. 154–155) After exploring this museum of 19th-century art, head next

CUSTOMIZING **YOUR DAY**

You may want to spend a morning or afternoon at the **Palace of Versailles** (see p. 127). Louis XIV's massive château and garden is about 40 minutes by train from central Paris. From St.-Michel-Notre Dame, Champ de Mars-Tour Eiffel, or any of the other RER stations between, take a C train to Versailles–Rive Gauche. It's a short walk from the station to the palace.

door to the ■ Musée National de la Légion d'Honneur (*2 rue de la Légion d'Honneur, 7th arr., www.legion dhonneur.fr, 01 40 62 84 25, closed Mon., Tues., Jan. 1, May 1, Aug. 15, Nov. 1, and Dec. 25*), which has displays on France's highest order of merit.

❹ Bateau Mouche Cruise (*www .bateaux-mouches.fr, 01 42 25 96 10, €€€*) After viewing the city from the river, watch for the ■ Flame of Liberty (northern end of Pont d'Alma), an 11-foot-tall (3.4 m) copy of the flame that's held by New York's Statue of Liberty. The monument, donated by the *Herald Tribune* in 1989, stands above the tunnel where Diana, Princess of Wales died in 1997. The flame became an unofficial memorial to the princess, although the city no longer allows people to leave tributes.

WHIRLWIND TOURS

Paris for Fun

*From sensuous sculpture to excellent shopping and foodie delights,
nothing says fun as much as a day in the city of light.*

❶ Musée Rodin (see pp. 26, 152–153) **An 18th-**
century château and its formal garden are home
to Auguste Rodin's best-known sculptures. Walk
down rue de Varenne toward St.-Sulpice.

❷ St.-Germain Shopping (see p. 26)
Whether you prefer your fashion classic
or hip, you'll find clothes and accessories
galore in the streets around St.-Germain
des-Prés and St.-Sulpice. Head east on
boulevard St.-Germain.

PARIS FOR FUN   DISTANCE: 3.3 MILES (5.3 KM)
TIME: APPROX. 8.5 HOURS   MÉTRO START: VARENNE

7 Café Panis (see p. 27) While away the rest of the evening enjoying a lovely Seine view and great people-watching.

6 Shakespeare and Company (see pp. 27, 67) Browse this historic bookstore, crammed with new and secondhand English-language books. Return to Quai Montebello and go east.

5 Maison de la Lozère (see p. 27) Enjoy the flavors of one of France's most rural regions at this specialty restaurant. Walk east along Quai St.-Michel and Quai Montebello.

Musée du Louvre

QUAI DU LOUVRE

PONT DU CARROUSEL

PONT NEUF

La Conciergerie

Ste.-Chapelle

St.-Michel

BLVD. ST.-GERMAIN

Le Comptoir

BLVD. ST.-MICHEL

Q. DE GESVRES

VOIE GEORGES POMPIDOU

Hôtel de Ville

QUAI DE L'HÔTEL DE VILLE

BLVD. DU PALAIS

(M) Cité

Île de la Cité

(M) Maison de la Lozère

5

Cathédrale de Notre-Dame de Paris

Shakespeare and Company

6 7 Café Panis

Île St.-Louis

(M) Cluny - La Sorbonne

Musée de Cluny

QUAI DE LA TOURNELLE

PONT DE SULLY

BLVD. ST.-GERMAIN

La Sorbonne

0 _____ 1 mile

0 _____ 1 kilometer

3 Le Comptoir (see p. 26) Lunch at this simple, elegant brasserie, which has a terrace for fine days. Walk west on boulevard St.-Germain, then turn north on rue des Sts.-Pères.

4 Left Bank Antiquing (see p. 27) Explore the antique collectors' paradise in rue de Seine, rue Bonaparte, and rue Jacob. Walk east along Quai Malaquais, Quai de Conti, and Quai des Grands Augustins.

The garden of the Musée Rodin is an inspiring place to start the day.

Musée Rodin

1 A Paris gem, this spectacular museum in the 18th-century Hôtel Biron displays many of Auguste Rodin's sculptures. The garden is a delight, filled with roses, peonies, boxwoods, hydrangeas, and many famous Rodin works, including "**The Thinker.**" The outdoor café is a good place for a coffee at the start the day.

79 rue de Varenne, 7th arr. • www.musee-rodin.fr • 01 44 18 61 10 • €€, garden only: € • Closed Mon., Jan. 1, May 1, and Dec. 25 • Métro: Varenne or Invalides

St.-Germain Shopping

2 Since the death of Yves St.-Laurent, Stefano Pilati has done an excellent job keeping **YSL** *(6 place St.-Sulpice, 6th arr.),* an iconic French brand, both chic and cutting edge. **agnès b.** *(6 and 10–12 rue du Vieux Colombier, 6th arr.)* is the place for affordable, simple, stylish fashion for the whole family. For unique pieces by French designers, including handbags, sunglasses, fashion, and art, drop into **Arty Dandy** *(1 rue de Furstemberg, 6th arr.).* There are stylish own-label creations and other originals at **Victoire** *(1 rue Madame, 6th arr.),* or, for a trendy French handbag or scarf, stop by **Petite Mendigote** *(23 rue du Dragon, 6th arr.).*

St.-Germain, 6th and 7th arr. • Closed Sun. • Métro: Sèvres-Babylone, St.-Sulpice, or St.-Germain des-Prés

Le Comptoir

3 Chef Yves Camdeborde presides over this Parisian institution, which is impossible to get into on weeknights, but by day and on weekends it's a delightful and delicious brasserie. Fancy a simple but elegant salad of greens and foie gras and a glass of rosé? This is the place. Seating outside on the terrace in fine weather is sublime.

9 carrefour de l'Odéon, 6th arr. • 01 44 27 07 97 • €€ • Métro: Odéon

Left Bank Antiquing

4 Rue de Seine, rue Bonapartre, rue Jacob, and rue de l'Université are good places for a stroll and some antique shopping. In this, an area known as the **Carré Rive Gauche,** there are more than a hundred antique and art dealers selling everything from beautiful pieces of primitive art to exquisite Louis XIV furniture.

www.carrerivegauche.com • Métro: Rue du Bac or St.-Germain des-Prés

Maison de la Lozère

5 Take a trip to the Lozère region of southeast France—where cattle roam and Roquefort is aged—without leaving Paris. Dine on *salade du Roquefort,* hearty brown bread, and *entrecôte de Lozère* (steak) accompanied by one of the region's wines. On Thursdays, the menu includes a dreamy *aligot,* the region's famous dish of creamed potatoes with Cantal cheese, which is hard to find anywhere else in the capital.

1 bis & 4 rue Hautefeuille, 6th arr. • www.lozere-a-paris.com • 01 43 54 26 64
• €€ • Closed Sun. • Reservations required • Métro: St.-Michel

Shakespeare and Company

6 Here is one of the most charming and bohemian English-language bookstores in the world. Countless writers have visited to browse and rest among the stacks. If you buy a book, get a cashier to emboss it with their famous "Shakespeare & Co. Kilometer Zero Paris" stamp on the way out, which makes for a great souvenir.

37 rue de la Bûcherie, 5th arr. • www.shakespeareandcompany.com • 01 43 25 40 93
• Métro: St.-Michel

Café Panis

7 Stop here for a *digestif* or a coffee while enjoying the terrace in good weather, with an excellent view of the Seine and Notre-Dame. From here you can watch rollerbladers do tricks and people wander by, or just gaze at the moon rising over Paris.

21 quai Montebello, 5th arr. • 01 43 54 19 71 • Métro: St.-Michel

Paris in a Weekend with Kids

Your first family day in Paris is packed with famous attractions, including one of the world's greatest art museums and the Tour Eiffel.

4 **Avenue des Champs-Élysées** (see pp. 30, 131) Take in the busy shops of Paris's most famed street and discover the Grand Palais's science museum. Continue west to the huge stone archway.

5 **Arc de Triomphe** (see pp. 31, 138–139) Napoleon's triumphal arch towers over the Étoile, the city's busiest traffic circle. Take the métro three stops to Trocadéro station.

6 **Tour Eiffel** (see pp. 31, 149) Climb the stairs or ride the elevator to the second floor of the iron tower, built in 1889 and still a symbol of France.

**PARIS WITH KIDS DAY 1   DISTANCE: 4.4 MILES (7 KM)
TIME: APPROX. 8 HOURS   MÉTRO START: PALAIS-ROYAL MUSÉE DU LOUVRE**

3 Au Nain Bleu (see p. 30)
Circus decor and an eclectic
selection set the city's oldest
and largest toy store apart
from its modern competitors.
Head west and turn left onto
rue Boissy d'Anglas.

2 Jardin des Tuileries
(see pp. 30, 118–119) Paris's
oldest park is filled with
statues, fountains, and a
fairground in the summer
months. Leave from the
park's western end, cross
the Place de la Concorde,
walk two blocks down rue
Royale, and turn left onto
boulevard Malesherbes.

1 Musée du Louvre
(see pp. 30, 122–125) See the
Egyptian mummies and other
wonders in this famous art
museum, which was once a
medieval castle. Exit via the
Carrousel entrance.

0 ————— 1 mile
0 ————— 1 kilometer

Musée du Louvre

1 Taking your kids to such a large museum can be daunting, yet it is worth it. Head to the **Egyptian mummies** (Ground Floor, Sully Wing) or the gory **Italian and French Renaissance Paintings** (Ground Floor, Denon Wing), before exploring the **medieval castle foundations** (Ground Floor, Sully Wing).

SAVVY **TRAVELER**

To avoid the Louvre's long lines, use the entrance at the Palais-Royal Musée du Louvre métro stop, rather than the main visitors' entrance.

Rue de Rivoli, 1st arr. • www.louvre.fr • 01 40 20 53 17 • €€ • Closed Tues., Jan 1, May 1, and Dec. 25 • Métro: Palais-Royal Musée du Louvre

Jardin des Tuileries

2 These gardens are a breath of fresh air after the museum; a place to picnic and run around. From June to late August, the **Fête de Foraine carnival** (see p. 17) takes over part of the gardens, complete with merry-go-round, Ferris wheel, and many other rides.

Rue de Rivoli, 1st arr. • Métro: Tuileries

Au Nain Bleu

3 Paris's oldest (1836) and largest toy store stocks a vast array of toys, games, clothing, and other youthful distractions such as wooden toy cars and an extensive doll collection.

5 blvd. Malesherbes, 8th arr. • www.aunainbleu.com • 01 42 65 20 00 • Closed Sun. • Métro: Concorde or Madeleine

Avenue des Champs-Élysées

4 Stroll down this tree-lined street, past chic shops, restaurants, and cafés. Look for the **Disney Store** *(No. 44),* or for some chocolate, try **Jadis et Gourmande** just off the avenue at 49 bis, avenue Franklin D. Roosevelt. For some hands-on learning, the **Palais de la Découverte** (see p. 135) is a superb science museum.

Ave. des Champs-Élysées, 8th arr. • Métro: Champs-Élysées Clemenceau

The fountains in the Louvre's courtyard are a good place to cool down on a hot day.

Arc de Triomphe

5 Kids, like adults, will be awed by the size of Napoleon's triumphal arch. They will also love the view from the roof and will no doubt be fascinated by the crazy Parisian traffic below.

Place Charles de Gaulle, 8th arr. • www.arcdetriompheparis.com • 01 55 37 73 77
• €€ • Closed May 8, July 14, and Nov. 11 (a.m.); Jan. 1, May 1, and Dec. 25 (all day)
• Métro: Charles de Gaulle Étoile

Tour Eiffel

6 End the day with an exciting ride up this giant iron landmark. The best views are had from the second level, but kids will probably want to test their nerve by going all the way to the top.

Parc du Champ de Mars, 5 ave. Anatole, 7th arr. • www.tour-eiffel.com • 08 92 70 12
39 • To second floor and top: €€, €€€; for stairs: € • Métro: Bir-Hakeim

Paris in a Weekend with Kids

The second day of your weekend with kids is brimming with modern art, medieval cathedrals, and a fabulous park.

❶ Cathédrale de Notre-Dame de Paris (see pp. 34, 48–49) From the first stone, laid in 1163, it took 180 years to build Europe's first great Gothic cathedral, whose gargoyles will leave kids spellbound. Head north on rue d'Arcole, then turn left onto Quai de la Corse along the Seine River.

❷ La Conciergerie (see pp. 34, 44–45) This 14th-century former royal palace was converted into a prison in 1391. Cross the Pont au Change, follow boulevard de Sébastopol north, and turn right onto rue Aubry le Boucher.

❸ Centre Pompidou (see pp. 34–35, 90–91) Thirty years after it opened, the building and its museums are still drawing oohs and aahs from visitors. From the plaza's northern end, follow rue Rambuteau to the back of the Pompidou, turn left onto rue Beaubourg and right onto impasse Berthaud.

Basilique du Sacré Coeur
Musée de Montmartre
PLACE DU TERTRE
RUE DE MAUBEUGE
RUE LA FAYETTE
Folies Bergère
Musée Grévin
BLVD. POISSONNIÈRE
RUE
Les Halles   Les Halle
Bourse de Commerce
PLACE D CHÂTEL
Châtelet
Pont Neuf
QUAI DE LA MÉGISSERIE
PONT NEUF
La Conciergerie ❷
BLVD. DU PALAIS
QUAI DE MONTEBELL
St.-Michel
Musée de Cluny
La Sorbonn
Panthéo

WHIRLWIND TOURS

**PARIS WITH KIDS DAY 2   DISTANCE: 4.3 MILES (7 KM)
TIME: APPROX. 8 HOURS   MÉTRO START: CITÉ**

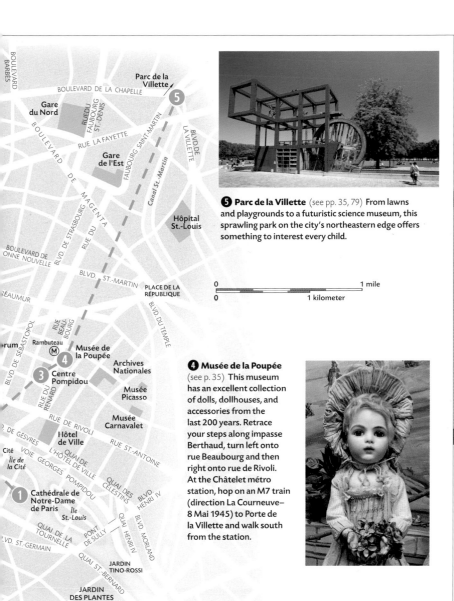

Parc de la Villette

5 Parc de la Villette (see pp. 35, 79) From lawns and playgrounds to a futuristic science museum, this sprawling park on the city's northeastern edge offers something to interest every child.

```
0                                    1 mile
0                    1 kilometer
```

4 Musée de la Poupée (see p. 35) This museum has an excellent collection of dolls, dollhouses, and accessories from the last 200 years. Retrace your steps along impasse Berthaud, turn left onto rue Beaubourg and then right onto rue de Rivoli. At the Châtelet métro station, hop on an M7 train (direction La Courneuve–8 Mai 1945) to Porte de la Villette and walk south from the station.

Cathédrale de Notre-Dame de Paris

1 Quasimodo, Victor Hugo's hunchbacked bell ringer, might be fictional, but the cathedral's gargoyles and chimeras are for real. Soaring pillars, massive stained-glass windows, and hundreds of flickering candles in the gargantuan interior bring the Middle Ages to life. The climax is climbing **the towers** and imagining Quasimodo and the beautiful gypsy Esmeralda hiding among the bells and flying buttresses, and looking down on Paris.

6 parvis de Notre-Dame, 4th arr. • www.notredamedeparis.fr
• 01 42 34 56 10 • Towers: €€, Treasury: €, Crypt: €
• Métro: Cité or St.-Michel

SAVVY **TRAVELER**

Paris has several permanent circuses, including the historic **Cirque d'Hiver** *(110 rue Amelot, 11th arr., 01 47 00 28 81, €€€€€)* near the Marais. Founded in 1852, the current shows include performing horses and tigers, magicians, acrobats, trapeze artists, and stunt bikes. And let's not forget the clowns.

La Conciergerie

2 The closest the city center comes to a medieval castle, this hulking structure was built by King Philippe the Fair in the 14th century as a royal palace, and it was later used as a notorious prison. Many who lost their heads to the guillotine during the French Revolution, including Queen Marie-Antoinette, were kept in these cold, stone cells before their deaths. Among the gruesome artifacts displayed inside are a **guillotine blade,** a **fountain** where the prisoners washed their clothes, a **stone table** where they ate, and the **Corner of the Last Good-byes,** where they boarded the tumbrel carts that took them to their execution. Needless to say, the Conciergerie is considered very haunted.

2 blvd. du Palais, 1st arr. • www.conciergerie.monuments-nationaux.fr
• 01 53 40 60 80 • €€ • Closed Jan. 1, May 1, and Dec. 25 • Métro: Cité or St.-Michel

Centre Pompidou

3 Kids will be fascinated by this multicolored, inside-out building, with a facade covered in pipes, ducts, and other functional features. Much of the interior is taken up by one of Europe's most important collections of modern and contemporary art. On the ground floor, check to see if there's anything on at the new **Children's Workshop**—an excellent space that holds various classes for six- to 12-year-olds. Also on the ground floor, the innovative **Galerie des Enfants** presents artistic exhibits and activities especially designed for kids. The outdoor spaces are just as dynamic: a cobblestone plaza that attracts Paris's best street performers and the **Igor Stravinsky Fountain** with its funky sculptures by artists Niki de Saint Phalle and Jean Tinguely.

Place Georges Pompidou, 4th arr. • www.centrepompidou.fr • 01 44 78 12 33 • Musée National d'Art Moderne: €€€ (first Sun. of the month: free) • Closed Tues. and May 1; Atelier Brancusi closed a.m. • Métro: Rambuteau or Châtelet

Musée de la Poupée

4 Rare and unusual dolls from the 19th century to the present day, including dolls from around the world and dolls made from unusual materials, fill this charming museum.

Impasse Berthaud, 3rd arr. • www.museedelapoupeeparis.com • 01 42 72 73 11 • €€ • Closed Mon. and public holidays • Métro: Rambuteau

Parc de la Villette

5 Creative urban renewal morphed an ugly 19th-century industrial area into a huge green space replete with lawns, playgrounds, and themed gardens designed especially for children. The park is known for its giant abstract structures that kids are free to climb all over. On the north side of the canal that runs through the park, **La Cité des Sciences et de l'Industrie** (*30 ave. Corentin Cariou, 01 40 05 70 00, €€, closed Mon.*) is a massive science museum packed with hands-on exhibits showcasing everything from space travel and natural disasters to the origins of life.

Ave. Jean Jaurès • Métro: Porte de la Villette or Pantin

La Cité des Sciences et de l'Industrie has one of France's biggest movie theaters.

PART 2

Paris's Neighborhoods

Station
Pont Cardinet

CIMETIÈRE
DE
MONTMARTRE

Moulin Rouge

AVENUE DE VILLIERS

BOULEVARD DES BATIGNOLLES

Gare
St.-Lazare

Musée
Cernuschi

PARC
MONCEAU

BLVD DE COURCELLES

AVENUE DE WAGRAM

RUE DE LA
PÉPINIÈRE

RUE ST.-LAZARE

BOULEVARD HAUSSMANN

Musée
Jacquemart-
André

AVENUE DE LA
GRANDE ARMÉE

PLACE
CHARLES
DE GAULLE

Ave. DE FRIEDLAND

La Défense

Arc de Triomphe   Lido

Champs-Élysées   **130**

Opéra
Garnier

Office du
Tourisme

AVENUE FOCH

AVENUE DES CHAMPS-ÉLYSÉES

PLACE DE LA
MADELEINE

BLVD. DES CAPUCINES

AVENUE VICTOR HUGO

La Madeleine

PLACE
VENDÔME

AVENUE D'IÉNA

AVENUE MARCEAU

Grand
Palais

Petit
Palais

PLACE DE LA
CONCORDE

RUE
ROYALE

AVENUE

Bois de
Boulogne

COURS
ALBERT 1er

Galerie Nationale du
Jeu de Paume

JARDIN DES
TUILERIES

St.-Roch

Palais de Tokyo

COURS LA REINE

Seine

The Louvre & Palais-Royal   **112**

D'ORSAY

QUAI

QUAI ANATOLE FRANCE

JARDINS
DU
TROCADÉRO

Musée du
Quai Branly

ESPLANADE
DES
INVALIDES

Assemblée
Nationale

Musée
d'Orsay

QUAI VOLTAIRE

AVE. DE NEW YORK

PONT DE
L'ALMA

P DES
INVALIDES

QUAI D'ORSAY

AVENUE BOSQUET

BLVD. DE LA
TOUR MAUBOURG

BLVD ST.-GERMAIN

Tour Eiffel

Les
Invalides

Tour Eiffel & Les Invalides   **144**

St.-Germain-
des-Prés

PONT DE
BIR-HAKEIM

PARC DU
CHAMP
DE MARS

AVE. DE TOURVILLE

Musée
Rodin

RUE DE VARENNE

BLVD.

BOULEVARD

École
Militaire

Hôtel
Matignon

RUE DE BABYLONE

St.-Sulpice

BOULEVARD

DE GRENELLE

AVE. DE LOWENDAL

AVE. DE BRETEUIL

BLVD DES INVALIDES

UNESCO

St.-Germain & Montparnasse   **70**

BLVD. GARIBALDI

JARDIN DU
LUXEMBOURG

★ **Paris**

RUE LECOURBE

BLVD PASTEUR

RUE DE VAUGIRARD

BLVD. DE VAUGIRARD

Tour
Montparnasse

BOULEVARD DU MONTPARNASSE

BLVD. RASPAIL

Gare
Montparnasse

CIMETIÈRE DU
MONTPARNASSE

RUE DU MAINE

RUE
FROIDEVAUX

PLACE
DENFERT
ROCHEREAU

0 ——————— 1 mile

0 ——————— 1 kilometer

Paris's Neighborhoods

Musée de Montmartre
Basilique du Sacré-Coeur
PLACE DU TERTRE

DE CLICHY

Montmartre **160**

Gare du Nord
RUE DE MAUBEUGE
RUE DE LA FAYETTE

RUE DU FAUBOURG ST.-DENIS
RUE DU FAUBOURG SAINT-MARTIN
BOULEVARD

Gare de l'Est

RUE DE CHÂTEAUDUN
RUE LA FAYETTE
RUE LA FAYETTE

Folies Bergère

Canal St.-Martin
BLVD. DE LA VILLETTE
BLVD DE LA VILLETTE

Hôpital St.-Louis

BLVD. MONTMARTRE
BLVD DES ITALIENS
BLVD. POISSONNIÈRE
BOULEVARD DE BONNE NOUVELLE
RUE DE STRASBOURG
RUE DU

BLVD. ST.-MARTIN
RUE DU 4 SEPTEMBRE
RUE RÉAUMUR
RUE ST.-MARTIN

PLACE DE LA RÉPUBLIQUE

PLACE DES VICTOIRES

Châtelet & Les Halles **82**

AVENUE DE LA RÉPUBLIQUE

Palais-Royal
Comédie Française
RUE DE RIVOLI

Les Halles
Bourse de Commerce Forum

Centre Pompidou

BLVD DE SÉBASTOPOL
RUE DU RENARD

Archives Nationales

BLVD DU TEMPLE
BOULEVARD

BOULEVARD RICHARD LENOIR
VOLTAIRE

Cimetière du Père-Lachaise

Musée du Louvre

Musée de l'Histoire de France
Musée Carnavalet

Musée Picasso

QUAI DU LOUVRE
QUAI DE LA MÉGISSERIE
PLACE DU CHÂTELET
RUE DE RIVOLI

Le Marais & Bastille **96**

PONT DES ARTS
PONT NEUF

La Conciergerie
Ste.-Chapelle

Q. DE GESVRES
VOIE GEORGES

Île de la Cité

Hôtel de Ville

L'HÔTEL DE VILLE
QUAI DE
QUAI DES CÉLESTINS

RUE ST.-ANTOINE

PLACE DES VOSGES

PLACE DE LA BASTILLE

RUE DU FAUBOURG ST.-ANTOINE

The Islands **40**

QUAI
DE MONTEBELLO

Cathédrale de Notre-Dame de Paris

POMPIDOU
Île St.-Louis

BLVD. HENRI IV
RUE DE LYON

ST.-GERMAIN

Musée de Cluny

QUAI DE LA TOURNELLE
PONT DE SULLY

QUAI HENRI IV
BLVD. MORLAND

AVE. LEDRU-ROLLIN
AVE. DAUMESNIL
DIDEROT

Palais du Luxembourg

BLVD. ST.-GERMAIN

La Sorbonne

Panthéon

Institut du Monde Arabe

RUE ST.-BERNARD

JARDIN TINO-ROSSI

PONT D'AUSTERLITZ

BOULEVARD

Gare de Lyon

Bois de Vincennes

BOULEVARD SAINT-MICHEL

Quartier Latin **54**

JARDIN DES PLANTES

QUAI DE LA RAPÉE
QUAI D'AUSTERLITZ

Grande Mosquée de Paris

Hôpital Val de Grâce

Musée National d'Histoire Naturelle

Gare d'Austerlitz

Seine

BLVD. DE BERCY

BOULEVARD DE PORT-ROYAL

BLVD. ST.-MARCEL

QUAI DE L'HÔPITAL

PONT DE BERCY
QUAI DE BERCY

BLVD. ST.-JACQUES

AVE. DES GOBELINS
BOULEVARD
BLVD. AUGUSTE BLANQUI
PLACE D'ITALIE

BOULEVARD VINCENT AURIOL

QUAI DE LA GARE

The Islands

Two islands in the Seine River—the Île de la Cité and Île St.-Louis—are at the heart of Paris's 2,000-year history. It was here that a Celtic tribe called the Parisii established a fishing village that evolved into a strategic Roman town, which in turn became the seat of the French kings and a hotbed of the revolution. The evidence of this rich history remains, from Cathédrale de Notre-Dame de Paris's towers and the stained glass of Ste.-Chapelle to the bastions of La Conciergerie prison and the 17th-century mansions that housed the leading figures of the Enlightenment. That bygone vibe endures in the Gothic churches, the flower market, the narrow streets of Île St. Louis, and the cloisters quarter beside Notre-Dame, where the 21st century still seems far, far away. The Conciergerie prison may now host guided tours, rather than prisoners on their way to the guillotine, but the islands retain their real-world power in institutions like the Palais de Justice. Away from the crowds, quiet parks and quayside perches provide places to sit and relax by the river.

◐ **The medieval Cathédrale de Notre-Dame de Paris replaced an earlier Christian basilica built at least five centuries before.**

The Islands

For a flavor of Paris, stroll the length of the Îles de la Cité and St.-Louis, where little has changed in 400 years.

① Square du Vert-Galant (see p. 44) Start beneath King Henri IV's bold equestrian statue overlooking the riverfront park that bears his nickname, then walk east to the Pont Neuf bridge.

② Pont Neuf (see p. 44) The city's oldest bridge leaps the Seine River in 12 elegant arches and a patch of terra firma at the Île de la Cité's western end. Remain on the island and walk east along Quai de l'Horloge. Turn right onto boulevard du Palais.

③ La Conciergerie (see pp. 44–45) Marie-Antoinette and Robespierre were among the thousands who started their journey to the guillotine from this palace turned prison. On leaving, turn right on boulevard du Palais.

**THE ISLANDS   DISTANCE: APPROX 1.5 MILES (2.4 KM)
TIME: APPROX. 5–6 HOURS   MÉTRO START: PONT NEUF**

THE ISLANDS

8 Île St.-Louis (see pp. 46–47) Now the home of Berthillon ice cream and specialty shops, the aristocratic island preserves its 17th-century architecture and timeless character. Head east to explore rue St.-Louis en l'Île.

7 Ancien Cloître Quartier (see p. 46) All that remains of the cloisters that once surrounded Notre-Dame is this tiny maze of streets along the Seine. From the park behind Notre-Dame, cross over the Pont St.-Louis.

6 Cathédrale de Notre-Dame de Paris (see pp. 48–49) France's most celebrated cathedral is every bit as imposing today as 700 years ago, a structure that was meant to both inspire and instill the fear of God. From the front of the cathedral, walk a block north along rue d'Arcole.

THE ISLANDS

5 Place Louis Lépine (see pp. 45–46) A flower market rules the square on weekdays, and on Sundays an equally colorful bird market takes place. Move a block down rue de la Cité to the cathedral square and its equestrian statue of Charlemagne.

4 Ste.-Chapelle (see p. 45) St. Louis built this Gothic masterpiece for Christian relics brought back from the Middle East during the 13th-century Crusades. Cross boulevard du Palais and walk a block down rue de Lutèce.

Square du Vert-Galant

1 Like the prow of a great ship, the square punctuates the downstream end of the Île de la Cité. Reached via stairs descending from street level, the leafy triangle is the only part of the island that lies at the original water level. The square is named for King Henri IV—dubbed the "Vert Galant" because of his dashing reputation as a lothario—whose **equestrian statue** is on the terrace at the top of the stairs. Legend has it that the large tree near the park's western end is the first in Paris to turn green in spring. It was here that Jacques de Molay, last grand master of the Knights Templar, was burned at the stake in 1314. Tour boats depart from the park's north shore.

Pont Neuf, 1st arr. • Métro: Pont Neuf

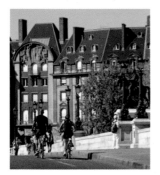

The Pont Neuf is popular as a thoroughfare and for enjoying views of the river.

Pont Neuf

2 Despite having a name meaning "New Bridge," this is the oldest of the city's many spans across the Seine River. Construction finished in 1607, and although restored many times, the bridge looks much the same as 400 years ago— seven arches on the north side of the island and five on the south, decorated with gargoyles and other grotesques. Pont Neuf's dreamy panoramas attract both photographers and lovers searching for the city's most romantic spot.

Île de la Cité, 1st arr. • Métro: Pont Neuf

La Conciergerie

3 In the midst of the French Revolution, the Reign of Terror (1793–1794) reached its cruelest extreme inside this notorious prison on the north shore of the Île de la Cité. Originally part of a medieval royal palace, the turreted structure was converted into a prison in the late 14th century. By the late 18th century, thousands of people were being tried, tortured, and detained inside, awaiting the executioner's blade. Queen Marie-Antoinette spent several months in captivity before her date with destiny, near the cells where revolutionary leaders Robespierre and Danton were later imprisoned before their own beheadings. The **Chapelle des Girondins**—where 22 revolutionaries spent their last night singing and dancing around the body of a dead comrade—is now a museum displaying Marie-Antoinette's crucifix and a guillotine blade, among other items.

2 blvd. du Palais, 1st arr. • www.conciergerie.monuments-nationaux.fr • 01 53 40 60 80 • €€ • Closed Jan. 1, May 1, and Dec. 25 • Métro: Cité or St.-Michel

Ste.-Chapelle

4 This delicate building—an exquisite former royal chapel—is an astonishing survivor among Paris's medieval architecture. It was commissioned by King Louis IX in the mid-13th century to house holy relics (such as the crown of thorns and pieces of the True Cross) that he had collected during the Crusades. (The relics are now kept in the treasury at Notre-Dame; see p. 49.) Along with the Conciergerie, the church is all that remains of the old Palais de la Cité, a former royal palace. The design is a mixture of flying buttresses, sumptuous woodwork, and dazzling ceilings. Original 13th-century stained-glass windows with 1,100 intricate biblical scenes transform the upper chapel into a translucent jewelry box. Ste.-Chapelle is enclosed within the **Palais de Justice,** a complex of 19th-century buildings that house the city's highest law courts.

4 blvd. du Palais, 1st arr. • www.sainte-chapelle.monuments-nationaux.fr • 01 53 40 60 80 • €€ • Closed Jan. 1, May 1, and Dec. 25 • Métro: Cité or St.-Michel

Place Louis Lépine

5 Named for a former police chief, this small square offers a splash of color amid the dour civic buildings that dominate the island's core. Tuesday through Saturday, an aromatic **flower market** takes over the space, dispensing a wide range of blooms, seeds, bulbs, and other gardening supplies. On Sundays, the square morphs into the **Marché aux Oiseaux** (Bird Market), where a wide variety of colorful birds and birdcages are sold.

Place Louis Lépine, 4th arr. • Métro: Cité

GOOD **EATS**

■ **LE FLORE EN L'ILE**
Delicious desserts and drinks, and dreamy views of Notre-Dame, make this riverside café the sort of place you want to linger for hours. **42 quai d'Orléans, 4th arr., 01 43 29 88 27, €€€**

■ **NOS ANCÊTRES LES GAULOIS**
A long-time Île St.-Louis favorite. The hearty fixed-price menu runs heavy on crudités and grilled meats, plus all the wine you can drink. **39 rue St.-Louis-en-l'Île, 4th arr., 01 46 33 66 07, €€€€**

■ **LA ROSE DE FRANCE**
An indoor/outdoor café near Pont Neuf. Salads are the house specialty, but French favorites from snails to crème brûlée are also featured. **24 place Dauphine, 1st arr., 01 43 54 10 12, €€€**

Cathédrale de Notre-Dame de Paris

6 See pp. 48–49.

6 parvis de Notre-Dame, 4th arr. • www.notre damedeparis.fr • 01 42 34 56 10 • Towers: €€, Treasury: €, Crypt: € • Métro: Cité or St.-Michel

Ancien Cloître Quartier

7 The warren of narrow lanes on the north side of Notre-Dame recalls the medieval urban landscape that once covered much of central Paris. Streets in the Ancient Cloister Quarter, such as **rue des Ursins** and **rue de la Colombe,** evoke a time when monks lived in the shadow of the great cathedral. **Rue Chanoinesse** is flanked by ancient clergymen's houses, as well as a newer building on the site of the dwelling *(No. 10)* where the tragic 12th-century love affair between Abélard and Héloïse allegedly played out.

Rue d'Arcole, 4th arr. • Métro: Cité or St.-Michel

Île St.-Louis

8 The petite Île St.-Louis floats beneath the radar of most visitors, a slice of the Parisian past that has somehow persevered. Originally used for grazing cattle, the marshy island was transformed in the 17th century into an aristocratic enclave, where many of the bright sparks of the Enlightenment lived, worked, or played. Although now heavily restored, most of the buildings date from that period, such as the **Hôtel de Lauzun** *(17 quai d'Anjou),* built in 1657,

THE ISLANDS

Historic town houses line rue St.-Louis en l'Île.

which was home to the poets Charles Baudelaire (1811–67) and
Théophile Gautier (1811–72), and the composer Richard Wagner
(1813–83). The unstable land means many of the old buildings have
subsided, or lean to the left or to the right. The island's only church,
St.-Louis-en-l'Île *(19 bis, rue St.-Louis en l'Île, 4th arr., 01 46 34 11
60, closed Mon.)* has several claims to fame, including an offbeat
three-aisle configuration and an outdoor iron clock. Crowned by
a narrow steeple that towers over the neighborhood, the baroque
structure took more than a century (1656–1765) to complete. It is
notable for its soaring Corinthian columns and grand organ, and as a
venue for concerts of sacred music. Nowadays, Parisians flock to the
island not so much for rich history as for the fruity ice cream scooped
at **Berthillon** *(29 rue St.-Louis en l'Île).*

Pont de Sully, 4th arr. • Métro: Pont Marie

Cathédrale de Notre-Dame de Paris

Rising above the Île de la Cité, the cathedral of Notre-Dame is an example of medieval architectural genius.

Decapitated by the Romans, St. Denis is depicted holding his head in the cathedral's left portal.

"And the cathedral was not only company for him, it was the universe; nay, more, it was nature itself," wrote French writer Victor Hugo in *The Hunchback of Notre-Dame*. Hugo was speaking of the fictional Quasimodo, but he might as well have been referring to all mankind and its reaction to the Parisian church, built between 1163 and 1345. Few buildings have a more fabled story than this cathedral, whose history blends fact and fiction, making Notre-Dame both an architectural landmark and a cultural icon.

THE FACADE

Looming over Place de Parvis Notre-Dame, the cathedral facade is one of the great works of Gothic artistry. The **rose window** takes pride of place in the center—notice how it forms a massive halo around the Virgin and Child sculpture group—but your eye is also drawn to massive portals that frame the three entrances. The **Portal of the Last Judgment,** which metaphorically opens the doors to the paradise within the cathedral, is flanked by the **Portal of the Virgin** (left) and the **Portal of St. Anne** (right). Running across the top of all three portals is the spectacular **King's Gallery,** with 28 statues of the ancient monarchs of Israel and Judea.

NAVE & CHANCEL

Even by today's standards, the cathedral's proportions are immense: The core is 427 feet long (130 m) and 115 feet high (35 m), flanked by 37 chapels and 75 giant stone pillars. Upwards of 9,000 people can worship within these hallowed walls. The massive rose windows and their glass bays are as tall as a six-story building. The south window, installed in 1260, was a gift from St. Louis.

IN **THE KNOW**

The cathedral's **Night Shows** (July–Oct.) offer a rare chance to visit the building after dark and view its history through sounds and projected images.

THE TOWERS

Realm of Victor Hugo's fictional bell-ringer Quasimodo, the cathedral's twin towers rise 226 feet (69 m) into the Parisian sky. Visitors access them from an entrance at the bottom of the north tower. But be prepared to climb. The **Chimera Gallery,** about two-thirds of the way up, is the place to get up close and personal with Notre-Dame's gargoyles. But the best views are from the South Tower's roof.

THE TREASURY

Sacred objects from the birth of Christianity through modern times are safeguarded in the cathedral's treasury, accessed via a chapel to the right (south) of the main altar. Among the more noteworthy items are a golden shrine for the **Crown of Thorns,** as well as a **wooden fragment and nail,** presumed to be from the cross on which Jesus was crucified.

THE ISLANDS

6 parvis de Notre-Dame, 4th arr. • www.notredamedeparis.fr • 01 42 34 56 10 • Towers: €€, Treasury: €, Crypt: € • Night Shows: free; dates and times vary • Métro: Cité or St.-Michel

Gothic Architecture

It may be hard to believe, but people once considered the Gothic architecture that we admire today to be ugly and retrograde. Renaissance pundits coined the term when trying to link a mode they considered lowbrow to the barbarian tribes that overran the Roman Empire. The Goths had nothing to do with the design that bears their name. It wasn't until the 19th century that Gothic architecture was seen as one of the great achievements of Western civilization.

The flying buttresses of Notre-Dame (above) can best be viewed from Square Jean XXIII, behind the cathedral. Ste.-Chapelle has one of the world's largest collections of stained glass (right).

Religious Powerhouses

The construction of St.-Denis (see p. 52) and Notre-Dame (see pp. 48–49) heralded the development of Gothic architecture in Paris in the early 12th century, when France had grown into a great power with an urge to express itself in grandiose buildings. This segued nicely with the Catholic Church's desire to create great temples to God, whereas the Romanesque style that had dominated from the ninth century limited height and decoration.

Building Tall

French architects and masons solved these engineering dilemmas with innovations that began around 1120—soaring arches, ribbed vaulting, and flying buttresses—the structural elements of Gothic architecture. Together these allowed for much taller structures, thinner walls, and larger windows, resulting in dazzling spaces filled with light. Add a touch of melodrama with gargoyles (waterspouts) and you have a startling new architectural form that swept across Europe.

THE ISLANDS

Gothic Masterpeices

The **Basilique St.-Denis** in what is now suburban Paris, became the first true Gothic building thanks to a 12th-century renovation that added many of the new structural and design elements to the original eighth-century building. The nave and ambulatory became prototypes for similar creations.

Notre-Dame soon followed, with construction work starting about two decades after St.-Denis's renovation. The first of Europe's great Gothic cathedrals, everything about Notre-Dame was designed to impress, inspire, and intimidate anyone who gazed upon her. Although smaller than the other two, the royal chapel of **Ste.-Chapelle** (see p. 45), built to house holy relics, is considered the apex of Gothic decoration in Paris.

GOTHIC **TERMS**

Flying buttress An arch that takes the weight of a vault or roof from the upper part of a wall to an outer support.

Gargoyle A waterspout projecting from a roof or parapet, often depicting a grotesque figure or creature.

Pointed arches These arches help support the roof's weight, allowing for thinner walls.

Rib vault A stone rib supporting a vaulted ceiling.

Rose window A circular window with ornamental tracery. The west rose window in Notre-Dame is 31 feet (9.4 m) in diameter.

Underground Paris

From Edgar Allan Poe and Victor Hugo to Anne Rice and her celebrated vampires, underground Paris has provided rich pickings for popular literature. But the city's subterranean world also has its factual side—royal tombs and Roman ruins, rat-infested sewers and solemn memorials.

■ BENEATH NOTRE-DAME
Notre-Dame's **Crypte Archéologique** (*7 parvis de Notre-Dame, 4th arr., www.carnavalet.paris.fr, 01 55 42 50 10, €, closed Mon. and public holidays*) contains the remnants of various structures that have stood on this spot over the last 2,000 years, including a Gallo-Roman house, medieval shops, and a fourth-century bathhouse. Directly behind Notre-Dame, the subterranean **Mémorial des Martyrs de la Déportation** (*Square de l'Île de France, 4th arr., 01 46 33 87 56*) is dedicated to the 200,000 French who perished in Nazi concentration camps during World War II. Opened in 1962, the striking design is intended to evoke feelings of doom and claustrophobia.

■ OTHER CHURCH CRYPTS
The city's churches have their own sunken charms. The **Panthéon** (*Place du Panthéon, 5th arr., 01 44 32 18 00,*

€€, closed public holidays) crypt is the last resting place for many a famous Parisian, including Victor Hugo, Marie Curie, Émile Zola, Jean-Jacques Rousseau, and Voltaire. The crypt beneath the **Basilique St.-Denis** (*1 place de la Légion d'Honneur, 7th arr., 01 48 09 83 54, €€, closed Jan. 1, May 1, and Dec. 25*) is said to contain the remains of King Louis XVI and Queen Marie-Antoinette, as well as an ossuary holding the bones exhumed from royal tombs during the French Revolution.

■ SKULLS & GRAFFITI
Hundreds of abandoned mine shafts lie beneath Paris's streets, forming an underground labrynth that has been used by secret societies, resistance movements, and raucous party animals for hundreds of years. Today, although most of these tunnels are strictly off-limits, a committed group of "cataphiles" defy the police to roam

The remains of around six million Parisians make the city's Catacombs an unusual attraction.

the network and express themselves away from society's glare. For visitors, the only accessible part of the network are the **Catacombes de Paris** (*1 ave. du Colonel Henri Roi-Tanguy, 14th arr., www.catacombes-de-paris.fr, 01 43 22 47 63, €€, closed Mon.*), which were created in the late 18th century when authorities decided to relocate all of the city's medieval cemeteries—and their thousands of corpses—to the abandoned quarries. Victims of the revolution were among the first new bodies to be buried beneath the streets. The subterranean trail leads past walls of human skulls and unusual graffiti. Self-guided tours commence from the Place Denfert-Rochereau, near the Jardin du Luxembourg (see pp. 75–76) on the Left Bank.

■ A STROLL IN THE SEWERS
Another underground attraction is the sprawling **Musée des Égouts** (Sewers Museum; *opposite 93 quai d'Orsay, 7th arr., 01 47 05 10 29, €, closed Thurs., Fri., Jan. 1, last three weeks in Jan., and Dec. 25*), entered from the Quai d'Orsay. Located in genuine sewage tunnels— with metal grates over the rushing water—the displays cover Paris sewers past, present, and future.

Quartier Latin

Although the name Latin Quarter refers to the lingua franca of the scholars
and teachers who began to congregate in this riverside neighborhood during
medieval times, it is also a throwback to the area's first urbanizers. The
Roman town of Lutetia (Lutèce) was founded on islands in the Seine, but
it soon overflowed to the left bank. Here the Romans built a forum, public
baths (Musée de Cluny), and an open-air arena (Arènes de Lutèce) where
gladiators battled. By the Middle Ages, abbeys
and monasteries dominated the area, creating
a cluster of scholarship and learning that by the
13th century had evolved into a university called
the Sorbonne. The French Revolution gutted
many of the quarter's religious buildings, but
the immense Panthéon was spared, transformed
into an eternal tribute to the French giants of
science, literature, and philosophy. Reflecting
the ever-changing character of Paris, the area
has also become a hub for the city's Muslim
residents, home to France's largest mosque, and
a thriving Arab art and culture center.

❶ **An eclectic mix of
cafés, bars, and
artisanal food stores
line the crooked,
close-packed streets
of the Quartier Latin.**

Quartier Latin

Encounter Roman ruins, botanical gardens, and 21st-century riverfront architecture on a stroll in the Latin Quarter.

❶ St.-Séverin (see p. 58) Gothic also comes in small packages, epitomized by the petite flamboyance of a church dedicated to a sixth-century hermit saint. Turn left out of the church, cross boulevard St.-Germain, and hang a quick right on rue Cluny.

❷ Musée de Cluny (see pp. 64–65) See Roman baths and a medieval mansion filled with artifacts from the Middle Ages in one of the city's best small museums. Cross the square in front of the museum, and follow rue de la Sorbonne along the west side of the university.

❸ La Sorbonne (see pp. 58–59) Many have found education and enlightenment within the walls of this hallowed university, founded in the 13th century as a theological college. Turn left on rue Cujas and continue to Place du Panthéon.

❹ Panthéon (see p. 59) This towering neoclassical church was converted during the revolution into a secular resting place for those who inspired France to greatness. Move one block east along Place du Panthéon.

❺ St.-Étienne-du-Mont (see p. 60) An elaborate rood screen dominates the nave of this simple yet sumptuous Gothic church. Walk two blocks east along rue Clovis, veer left on rue du Cardinal Lemoine and then right on rue Monge.

**QUARTIER LATIN   DISTANCE: 4 MILES (6.4 KM)
TIME: APPROX. 6–8 HOURS   MÉTRO START: ST.-MICHEL**

❾ Institut du Monde Arabe
(see p. 63) The Arab World Institute's ultramodern building is nearly as impressive as the Islamic art and culture displayed within one of the world's foremost centers of Arabic learning.

❽ Jardin des Plantes (see pp. 62–63) The city's botanical gardens blend flora, fauna, and museums. Exit the gardens via the Place Valhubert gate, and turn left on Quai St.-Bernard.

❼ Grande Mosquée de Paris
(see pp. 61–62) The mosque is a dazzling display of North African architecture. Cross rue Geoffroy St.-Hilaire to the gardens across the road.

❻ Arènes de Lutèce (see pp. 60–61) Gladiatorial combat once took center stage at this ancient Roman arena, now a quiet park. On leaving, turn left on rue Lacépède and then right on rue Geoffroy St.-Hilaire.

QUARTIER LATIN

St.-Séverin

1 Despite its diminutive size, the Latin Quarter's parish church embraces a long and incredibly rich history. Its patron saint was a sixth-century hermit monk who lived in Paris around the time that King Clovis decided to convert to Christianity and, in so doing, forever changed the fortunes of both the city and France. Construction of the current church was a protracted affair that commenced in the 13th century with the facade and nave, and ended in the 17th century when the cousin of King Louis XIV (Mademoiselle de Montpensier) hired royal architect Charles Le Brun to "modernize" the interior. He was careful to preserve the church's Flamboyant Gothic spirit, manifested in its copious **stained glass,** menacing **gargoyles,** and a **double ambulatory** lined with pillars that bear an uncanny resemblance to palm trees. St.-Séverin's steeple shelters the oldest **bell** in Paris (1412). The courtyard on the south side was once the parish burial ground; the cloister-like structure along the outer side is the city's only remaining charnel house. The church often hosts Saturday night **concerts.**

One of a series of stained-glass windows by Jean-René Bazaine, installed between 1964 and 1969 in the church of St.-Séverin

3 rue des Prêtres St.-Séverin, 5th arr. • www.saint-severin.com • 01 42 34 93 50 • Métro: Cluny La Sorbonne or St.-Michel

Musée de Cluny

2 See pp. 64–65.

6 place Paul Painlevé, 5th arr. • www.musee-moyenage .fr • 01 53 73 78 00 • €€ • Closed Tues., Jan. 1, May 1, and Dec. 25 • Métro: Cluny La Sorbonne or St.-Michel

La Sorbonne

3 One of the world's oldest and most prestigious institutes of learning, the Sorbonne traces its origins to the mid-13th century, when canon Robert de Sorbon (confessor to King Louis IX) created a theological college for poor students. From those humble beginnings rose today's campus, where more than 23,000 students and 1,300 teachers labor in 17 departments. Cardinal Richelieu oversaw construction of the present building during his tenure as the university's chancellor in the early 17th century. The main building is a maze of lecture halls and laboratories, **libraries** and offices, an **observatory,** and a Jesuit-style **church** where Richelieu is buried.

1 rue Victor Cousin, 5th arr. • www.english.paris-sorbonne.fr • 01 40 46 22 11 • Group tours only: minimum ten people, reservation required • Métro: Cluny La Sorbonne

Panthéon

4 Many French movers and shakers found their last resting spot inside this soaring Latin Quarter edifice. Although erected as a church dedicated to St. Genevieve, the massive structure was secularized during the revolution and transformed into a temple to fame where influential Frenchmen were buried. Among those interred within the **crypt** are philosophers Voltaire, Descartes, and Rousseau, writers Victor Hugo, Émile Zola, and Alexandre Dumas, inventor Louis Braille, and Nobel Prize-winning scientist Marie Curie (one of only two women buried there). Built from 1758 to 1789, the Panthéon was an early example of neoclassical architecture, with a facade modeled on the original Pantheon in Rome and a cavernous interior in the shape of a Greek cross. The ellipsoidal dome influenced the design of the U.S. Capitol Building.

Place du Panthéon, 5th arr. • www.pantheonparis.com • 01 44 32 18 00 • €€ • Closed Jan. 1, May 1, and Dec. 25 • Métro: Cardinal Lemoine

GOOD **EATS**

■ **COCO DE MER**
Located just south of the Jardin des Plantes, this exotic restaurant serves Seychelles cuisine sourced from the middle of the Indian Ocean. Swordfish vindaloo and octopus curry are favorites. **34 blvd. St.-Marcel, 5th arr., 01 47 07 06 64, €€€**

■ **NOURA**
This airy rooftop restaurant at the Institut du Monde Arabe serves up fabulous Lebanese cuisine with dreamy views down the Seine to Notre-Dame. **1 rue des Fossés St.-Bernard, 5th arr., 01 55 42 55 42, €€€**

■ **LE RIBOULDINGUE**
Just across the river from Notre-Dame, this tiny bistro serves hearty French country food such as tripe, pig's snout, and lamb's brain. If you find offal awful, opt for the fresh fish or veal steak. **10 rue St.-Julien-le-Pauvre, 5th arr., 01 46 33 98 80, €€€**

St.-Étienne-du-Mont

5 Literally within the shadow of the much larger Panthéon, St.-Étienne, one of the many beautiful churches on the Left Bank, is often overlooked. However, it contains one item unique in Paris: an elegant stone **rood screen** across the middle of the nave. A common feature in Gothic churches, the rood screen separated the chancel or high altar from the congregation and provided an extra surface on which to hang Christian imagery or a large rood (crucifix). Most were demolished during the Counter-Reformation, but St.-Étienne's rood screen survived into the modern era. Like so many of the city's churches, this one is a hybrid of styles, one of the last Gothic churches erected in Paris and one of the first with Renaissance influence. Although it is hard to see amidst the urbanization, the church crowns a hill *(mont)* named for Paris patron St. Genevieve and once adjoined a great abbey also dedicated to her memory. The abbey (and St. Genevieve's tomb) was destroyed during the anti-religious fervor that accompanied the revolution. Her **sarcophagus stone,** containing several relics, now rests inside St.-Étienne. The celebrated French playwright Jean Racine and the mathematician/philosopher Blaise Pascal are both buried here. The church's 17th-century organ is the focus of a year-round Saturday night concert series.

1 place Ste.-Geneviève, 5th arr. • 01 43 54 11 79 • Métro: Cardinal Lemoine

IN **THE KNOW**

A pastiche of Parisian life, **rue Mouffetard** traces the route of a Roman road through the Latin Quarter. First and foremost it is an outdoor food market where you can pick up all the ingredients you need for a picnic in the Jardin du Luxembourg or Jardin des Plantes (Botanical Gardens). "La Mouff" also attracts street performers, as well as those who relish moody neighborhood bars like **Requin Chagrin** (No. 10) and **Le Verre à Pied** (No. 118). Ernest Hemingway lived and wrote much of A Moveable Feast at **74 rue du Cardinal Lemoine,** just off Mouffetard.

Arènes de Lutèce

6 Nowadays, on a spot where gladiators once waged mortal combat, elderly men play *pétanque* (boules) among the remains of a Roman arena near the Jardins des Plantes (Botanical Gardens, see p. 62). Badly damaged when barbarians sacked Paris

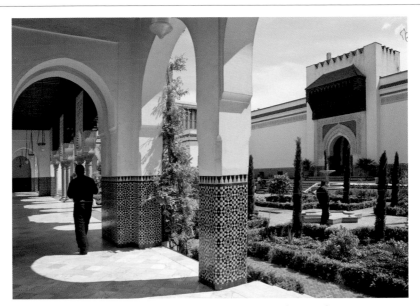
The Grande Mosquée's tranquil garden is a good place to escape the area's busy streets.

in the late third century, the arena lay buried and forgotten for nearly 1,500 years until its accidental discovery in 1869. Since then, the open-air stadium has been partially excavated and reconstructed. Estimates put its bygone capacity at 10,000 to 17,000 spectators, who crowded into the stone bleachers to watch sporting events, circus acts, and theater productions. Among the ruins are barred **animal cages** and a **stone stage** with acoustical niches used to amplify dialogue during plays or speeches.

47 rue Monge, 5th arr. • Métro: Cardinal Lemoine, Jussieu, or Place Monge

Grande Mosquée de Paris

7 Bringing a touch of North Africa to central Paris, the Grand Mosque comes as something of a visual shock after the Gothic architecture that dominates so much of the quarter. The elegant

Mudejar design permeates the complex, from the horseshoe arches and decorative tiles to the peaceful patios of the **garden**—which anyone can visit—the octagonal dome, and a 108-foot (33 m) minaret that towers above the neighborhood. France's largest place of Islamic worship was created in the early 1920s to express the nation's thanks to the hundreds of thousands of Muslims from the colonies who fought (and often died) alongside French troops in World War I. The materials and decorations—Lebanese cedar, North African copper, Persian carpets—were sourced throughout the Muslim world. During World War II, the mosque's mufti is credited with saving scores of local Jews from deportation to the Nazi death camps by giving them Muslim identification documents. The mosque's **hammam** (Turkish bath; *39 rue St.-Hilaire, 01 43 31 38 20, contact@lamosqueedeparis.com, Tues. and Sun, men only; Mon., Wed., Thurs., and Sat., women only*) is open to the public regardless of faith. The complex has a **restaurant** serving Middle Eastern cuisine and a small **souk** (market) offering North African arts and crafts.

2 bis, place du Puits de l'Ermite, 5th arr. • www.la-mosquee .com • 01 45 35 97 33 • € • Closed to visitors Fri. and Muslim holidays • Métro: Place Monge, Censier Daubenton, or Jussieu

Jardin des Plantes

8 This diverse green space on the eastern edge of the Latin Quarter does double duty as a crowd pleaser and serious research institute. The 69 acres (28 ha) of the Jardin des Plantes (Botanical Gardens) has enough to keep visitors busy for hours, especially those with smaller children. The **Ménagerie** is one of the world's oldest zoos, begun during the revolution with animals confiscated from the royal collection at Versailles. It is home to more than 1,000 animals, including rare red pandas and clouded leopards.

The romantic Rose Garden in the Jardin des Plantes blooms to perfection in May and June.

The garden is also home to the **Musée National d'Histoire Naturelle.** Don't miss the long procession of life-size stuffed animals crossing a re-creation of the African savanna in the museum's **Grande Galerie de l'Évolution** (Evolution Gallery) or the skeletons of huge dinosaurs and birds in the **Galerie de Paléontologie** (Palaeontology Gallery). Plant-lovers will enjoy the gardens' world-class botanical collection, especially the **Alpine Garden's** 2,000 or more species from the Alps, Pyrenees, and Himalaya, and the **Rose Garden's** 170 varieties. The newly renovated glass-and-steel **Grandes Serres** (greenhouses) include a display of tropical plants from New Caledonia. And make sure you find your way to the gazebo at the center of the hilly, yew-hedged **maze** for some great views over Paris.

Entrances on rue Geoffroy St.-Hilaire, rue Cuvier, and Quai St.-Bernard, 5th arr. • www.mnhn.fr • 01 40 79 56 01 • Greenhouses, zoo, and museums: €–€€ • Closed Tues. and May 1 • Métro: Gare d'Austerlitz, Censier Daubenton, or Jussieu

Institut du Monde Arabe

9 A striking contrast to the traditional design of the Grand Mosquée (see pp. 61–62), the Institut du Monde Arabe (Arab World Institute) is an unapologetically modern structure erected in the 1980s as a center for Arab and Islamic culture and studies. The southern facade of architect Jean Nouvel's masterpiece is clad in a massive **glass-and-metal screen** with geometric motifs that function as light-sensitive apertures, controlling how much sunlight penetrates into the building. The institute contains a library; an auditorium where music, dance, and theater are performed; and three floors of **museum** space showing artifacts both modern and ancient from around the Arab world. Taking pride of place on the top (ninth) floor is a Lebanese restaurant (see Good Eats, p. 59) and a **terrace** with fantastic views.

1 rue des Fossés St.-Bernard, 5th arr. • 01 40 51 38 38 • Museum: €€ • Closed Mon. • Métro: Jussieu, Cardinal Lemoine, or Place Monge

SAVVY **TRAVELER**

Slightly upstream from the Institut du Monde Arabe (Arab World Institute), on the Quai St.-Bernard, is **Jardin Tino Rossi.** This waterfront sculpture garden features works by international artists. On summer evenings, the space hosts free open-air dance lessons ranging from salsa and tango to hip-hop.

QUARTIER LATIN

Musée de Cluny

This architectural complex blends Gothic town house, Roman baths, and whimsical medieval garden.

"The Promenade," a 500-year-old *mille fleurs* ("thousand flowers") tapestry

Officially it is called the Musée National du Moyen Âge (National Museum of the Middle Ages), but Parisians are much more likely to use a simpler appellation—Musée de Cluny. This Left Bank compound was owned by the avid art collector and amateur archaeologist Alexandre du Sommerard in the early 19th century. On his death in 1842, the state purchased his house and collection and turned them into an outstanding museum of medieval art, including tapestries, sculptures, stained glass, gold and ivory objects, and furniture.

The Town House

Although based at Cluny in eastern France, the politically astute abbots kept a Parisian residence in the 14th century to be close to the royal court and the nearby university. The current structure, dubbed the Hôtel de Cluny, is largely the work of late 15th-century abbot Jacques d'Amboise. The meticulously restored manse—featuring decorative turrets, crenellated walls, and steeply pitched roofs with dormers—is an outstanding example of Gothic architecture, in particular the **chapel** and its French Flamboyant style vaulting (Room 20).

Medieval Treasures

The museum's forte is the decorative arts of the Middle Ages and especially its rich collection of tapestries. One highlight among the works is "**The Lady and the Unicorn**" series of six tapestries displayed beneath the central rotunda (Room 13). They were woven in the Netherlands between 1484 and 1500 using wool and silk threads. Five of them each depict one of the senses; the sixth alludes to sensuality and bears the inscription "To my only desire."

DON'T **MISS**

The gardens of the Hôtel de Cluny have changed many times since first planted in the 15th century, most recently in 2000, when they were reworked along whimsical medieval lines. The **Unicorn Forest** was inspired by the celebrated tapestries, and a **kitchen garden** is stocked with herbs and vegetables that would have been popular in the Middle Ages. The **flower meadow** takes its cue from the museum's *mille fleurs* ("thousand flowers") tapestries.

Roman Baths

The bathhouse forming part of the ground floor was developed between the first and third centuries A.D., when Paris was a thriving Gallo-Roman town. Given the maritime motifs, the baths were probably constructed by the guild of Paris boatmen, and it is believed they were later destroyed by invading barbarians. The *frigidarium* (cold water bath; Room 9) houses artifacts from antiquity—seek out the **Sailors' Pillar** and the fragment of a mosaic, "**Love Riding a Dolphin.**" Remains of a *tepidarium, caldarium,* and gymnasium are also visible.

6 place Paul Painlevé, 5th arr. • www.musee-moyenage.fr • 01 53 73 78 00 • €€ • Closed Tues., Jan. 1, May 1, and Dec. 25 • Métro: Cluny La Sorbonne or St.-Michel

QUARTIER LATIN

Existentialists & Intellectuals

The Left Bank is famous as a haunt of disaffected intellectuals, aspiring writers, and bohemian artists. This reputation was mostly earned between the 1920s and the 1950s, from the era of America's "Lost Generation" to the high tide of French existentialism. Attracted by the freedom of expression that prevailed in Paris, writers from France and abroad colonized the bars, cafés, and salons and drew inspiration from their adopted city.

Philosopher, feminist theorist, and writer Simone de Beauvoir (above); Shakespeare and Company (right), a magnet for booklovers

Writers' Enclave

American, English, and Irish writers flocked to Paris in the 1920s, including Ezra Pound, James Joyce, Ernest Hemingway, F. Scott Fitzgerald, Jean Rhys, Henry Miller, and George Orwell. They were drawn by the freedom and mental stimulation the city offered. Banned in their home countries, books such as Joyce's scatological masterpiece *Ulysses* (1922) and Miller's sexually explicit *Tropic of Cancer* (1934) could be printed and read in Paris.

Montparnasse Café Life

Support for aspiring writers was provided by American expatriates such as Sylvia Beach (see sidebar, opposite) and the fiercely modernist Gertrude Stein, who held a salon on rue de Fleurus, by the Jardin du Luxembourg. But the hub of intellectual life at this period lay in the cafés of Montparnasse, particularly **La Rotonde** *(105 blvd. du Montparnasse, 14th arr.)* and **Le Dôme** *(No. 108)*. Hemingway wrote most of *The Sun Also Rises* at a table in **La Closerie des Lilas** *(No. 171)*.

St.-Germain Celebrities

After the German occupation of 1940 to 1944, the focus of intellectual café life shifted northward to St.-Germain. At **Les Deux Magots** *(6 place St.-Germain-des-Prés, 6th arr.)* or **Café de Flore** *(172 blvd. St.-Germain, 6th arr.)*, the writers and philosophers Jean-Paul Sartre and Simone de Beauvoir held court as superstars of the trendsetting existentialist movement. In the postwar years they became the figureheads of a self-consciously disillusioned generation.

Today, the Left Bank cafés are still the natural habitat of many French intellectuals and writers, but they are considerably overwhelmed in numbers by the tourist hordes.

SHAKESPEARE & COMPANY

American Sylvia Beach established the English-language bookshop Shakespeare and Company in 1919. Her premises at 12 rue de l'Odéon, 6th arr., were a haven for expatriate writers in the 1920s and 1930s. Beach's bookshop closed in 1941, but its name and tradition are maintained in the current Shakespeare and Company across the Pont au Double from Notre-Dame cathedral *(37 rue de la Bûcherie, 5th arr.)*.

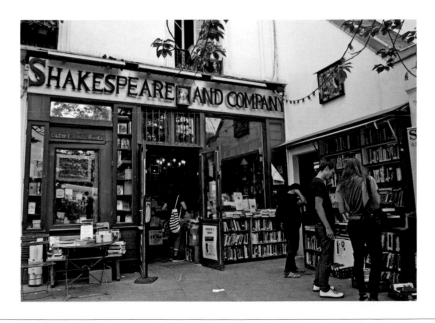

High-end Dining

Haute cuisine is alive and well in Paris, and visitors have a plethora of celebrated destinations to choose from. The chefs at these legendary restaurants have garnered 16 Michelin stars between them. A meal at one of their tables is not just lunch or dinner: It's an unforgettable experience.

QUARTIER LATIN

■ LA TOUR D'ARGENT

André Terail took over this historic restaurant in the Latin Quarter, with its unrivaled view over the Seine and Notre-Dame, when his father Claude—a legend—died in 2006. He has injected the restaurant with new energy while maintaining many of its traditions, including the famous *canard Tour d'Argent* (pressed duck), *quenelles de brochet* (pike quenelles), and a superb wine list.

15 Île de la Cité de la Tournelle, 5th arr., 01 43 54 23 31, €€€€€

■ LE MEURICE

The rococo dining room of Le Meurice, close to the Louvre, answers the question: What if Philippe Starck had designed Versailles? But it's Yannick Alleno's stunning compositions that leave diners in awe. The *"Terroir Parisien"* lunch menu is a delicious, high-end tribute to regional products

and traditions; the eight-course tasting menu is the meal of a lifetime.

228 rue de Rivoli, 1st arr., 01 44 58 10 10, €€€€€

■ PIERRE GAGNAIRE

Chef Pierre Gagnaire has addresses around the world but still considers his eponymous restaurant north of the Champs-Élysées *"le coeur"*—the heart. The dining room is insulated from the outside world, elegant but subdued, with little to distract from the overwhelming series of inventive dishes that will cross your table, from the first amuse-bouche to the last sweet *mignardise*.

6 rue Balzac, 8th arr. 01 58 36 12 50, €€€€€

■ LEDOYEN

This regal, neoclassical pavilion near the Champs-Élysées is a temple of gastronomy. The first restaurant here

At L'Arpège, Alain Passard brings a delicate touch to the cooking of simple ingredients.

appeared in 1779, when cows still grazed the area. Since then, it has fed royalty, literati, and high society. Current chef Christian LeSquer regales diners with classically rooted cooking that befits the luxe, romantic setting.

1 ave. Dutuit, 8th arr., 01 53 05 10 01, €€€€€

■ L'ARPÈGE

Alain Passard's sublime vegetables come direct from his own farm, but there's nothing rustic about a meal at L'Arpège, near Les Invalides. Yes, there is meat, fish, and fowl on the menu, but it's Passard's celebration of produce from the kitchen garden that has made him among the most influential chefs of the day.

84 rue de Varenne, 7th arr., 01 47 05 09 06, €€€€€

■ L'ASTRANCE

The least formal of Paris's three-star restaurants is near the Trocadero. There's room for only 25 diners in the high-ceilinged room, the theater for chef Pascal Barbot's imaginative, direct cooking. His signature galette of shaved raw *champignons de Paris* studded with *verjus*-marinated foie gras is a new classic.

4 rue Beethoven, 16th arr., 01 40 50 84 40, €€€€€

ST.-GERMAIN &
MONTPARNASSE

St.-Germain &
Montparnasse

An artistic flair still prevails in these two neighborhoods that stretch south from the Seine to the Cimetière du Montparnasse, whose tombstones commemorate the famous writers, artists, philosophers, and intellectuals who once frequented the area's cafés and gardens. Today, although the lively atmosphere of St.-Germain promises trendy shops and chic boutiques, you can still feel its creative history in the museums housing work by artists Eugène Delacroix and Ossip Zadkine. Enjoy a break from the hubbub with a stroll around the Jardin du Luxembourg, Paris's most popular park. The churches of St.-Germain-des-Prés and St.-Sulpice abound with interesting history and architecture. For a great view, head to the 56th floor of the Tour Montparnasse.

◉ **Les Deux Magots in the shadow of Église St.-Germain-des-Prés is a popular watering hole.**

St.-Germain & Montparnasse

Explore the parks and galleries of Paris's intellectual heart.

❶ Musée Delacroix (see p. 74) Romantic artist Eugène Delacroix's apartment and studio, along with his private garden, are tucked away in one of Paris's charming small squares. Walk south on rue de Furstemberg, then west on rue de l'Abbaye.

❷ Église St.-Germain-des-Prés (see p. 74) Once a sixth-century Benedictine abbey, Paris's oldest church has seen plenty of history. Walk south on rue Bonaparte.

❸ Église St.-Sulpice (see p. 75) Eugène Delacroix's murals decorate this large church, which also has one of the world's finest organs. Walk west on rue du Vieux Colombier, then turn south onto rue de Sèvres.

8 Tour Montparnasse (see p. 77) The 360-degree view of Paris from the 56th floor of this skyscraper is spectacular.

7 Cimetière du Montparnasse (see pp. 76–77) The final resting place for writers, artists, philosophers, musicians, and actors. Exit the cemetery at the northern entrance, and walk west on boulevard Edgar Quinet.

4 La Grande Épicerie de Paris (see p. 75) This is not a mere grocery store, but a gastronomic treasure trove of thousands of gourmet items. Walk south on rue de l'Abbé Grégoire, then east on rue de Vaugirard.

5 Jardin du Luxembourg (see pp. 75–76) Enjoy the hundreds of trees, flowers, statues, and fountains of the city's favorite park. Exit at the southwest corner, then walk southeast on rue d'Assas.

6 Musée Zadkine (see p. 76) This museum houses a collection of work by Russian-born sculptor and artist Ossip Zadkine. Walk southwest on rue Joseph Bara, turn right and then left onto rue de Chevreuse. Turn right onto boulevard du Montparnasse and then south on rue Huyghens.

ST.-GERMAIN & MONTPARNASSE DISTANCE: APPROX 3.1 MILES (5 KM)
TIME: APPROX. 6–7 HOURS MÉTRO START: ST.-GERMAIN-DES-PRÉS

Musée Delacroix

1 The Romantic artist Eugène Delacroix moved here in 1857 to work at the nearby Église St.-Sulpice (see opposite), where he painted murals that cemented his reputation as one of France's foremost artists. The museum, which became a national site in 1971, includes the painter's apartment, studio, and private garden. The paintings, pastels, watercolors, drawings, and sketches on display, from the **"Magdalene in the Desert,"** one of his most acclaimed works, to the **"Self-Portrait as Ravenswood,"** one of his few paintings of himself, represent almost every phase of his creativity. Memorabilia including easels, art palettes, the artist's personal letters, and items from his Morocco trip are on display. You can also walk around his much loved garden.

6 rue de Furstemberg, 6th arr. • www.musee-delacroix.fr • 01 44 41 86 50 • Closed Tues., Jan. 1, May 1, and Dec. 25 • € • Métro: St.-Germain-des-Prés or Mabillon

GOOD **EATS**

■ **LE CAFÉ DE LA MAIRIE**
Close to St.-Sulpice, the café offers sandwiches and hot meals.
8 place St.-Sulpice, 6th arr., 01 43 26 67 82, €€

■ **LA COUPOLE**
This atmospheric brasserie is near the Jardin du Luxembourg.
102 blvd. du Montparnasse, 14th arr., 01 43 20 14 20, €€€

■ **WADJA**
This bistro near the Jardin du Luxembourg serves hearty classic dishes that are wallet-friendly.
10 rue de la Grande-Chaumière, 6th arr., 01 46 33 02 02, €€

Église St.-Germain-des-Prés

2 Founded in 542 by King Childebert, Paris's oldest church was once part of a powerful and rich abbey. The current building, dating from the 11th century, retains some its **sixth-century columns**—part of an interior that includes Gothic vaulting and Romanesque arches. The abbey closed during the French Revolution after a mob stormed its prison during the September Massacres, when many suspected counter revolutionaries were killed. Gunpowder was later stored in the abbey, which exploded in 1794, destroying many of its buildings; the church was heavily restored in the 19th century. The dimly lit building holds the **tomb of René Descartes** (1596–1650), the father of modern philosophy.

3 place St.-Germain-des-Prés, 6th arr. • 01 55 42 81 33 • Métro: St.-Germain-des-Prés

Église St.-Sulpice

3 The building of Paris's second largest church (after Notre-Dame; see pp. 48–49) began in 1646 and took more than a hundred years. Three glorious Eugène Delacroix murals—**"Jacob Wrestling an Angel," "St. Michael Killing the Dragon,"** and **"Heliodorus Driven from the Temple"**—adorn the chapel to the right of the door. The church also houses one of the city's largest **organs,** whose 6,588 pipes fill the air with music after Sunday Mass.

Place St.-Sulpice, 6th arr. • 01 46 33 21 78 • Métro: St. Sulpice

The church of St.-Sulpice was the site of French writer Victor Hugo's wedding.

La Grande Épicerie de Paris

4 Foodie or not, everyone will appreciate this mammoth store full of gourmet delights. Twenty bakers and twenty-five pastry chefs produce buttery croissants, 70 specialty breads, artistic éclairs, petit fours, and dozens of other pastries every morning. You'll also find hot and cold cuisine from around the world, 57 kinds of bottled water, dozens of olive oils, and hundreds of cheeses. Don't forget the **wine cellar** either.

38 rue de Sèvres, 7th arr. • www.lagrandeepicerie.fr • 01 44 39 81 00 • Closed Sun., Jan. 1, Easter Mon., Aug. 15, and Dec. 25 • Métro: Sèvres-Babylone

Jardin du Luxembourg

5 This 60-acre (2.4 ha) oasis of greenery adjacent to the Luxembourg Palace (home of the French Senate) is Paris's favorite park. Queen Marie de Médicis constructed the garden and palace in the early 17th century to replicate her childhood home in Florence. Today, elm trees, apple and pear orchards, and formal flower beds fill the park, along with more than a hundred statues, including a small study of the **Statue of Liberty.** The **Médicis Fountain** is one of

ST.-GERMAIN & MONTPARNASSE

IN **THE KNOW**

Montparnasse (Mount Parnassus) takes its name from the mythical home of the Greek gods. Once the haunt of poetic students, the original hill was flattened in 1725. The area became known for cabarets and bohemian cafés that attracted struggling artists and writers such as Pablo Picasse, Marc Chagall, Ernest Hemingway, F. Scott Fitzgerald, and James Joyce.

the most beautiful water features in Paris. The park is a great place for kids, who enjoy sailing model boats on the octagonal pond. The play area includes pony rides, an old-fashioned puppet show, and even a classic merry-go-round.

Blvd. St.-Michel, 6th arr. • 01 42 64 33 99 • Métro: St.-Placide

Musée Zadkine

6 Around 300 sculptures from Russian-born 20th-century artist Ossip Zadkine are on display at his former cottage home. He gained an international reputation with his cubist-inspired and abstract sculpture, culminating in his famous "The Destroyed City," a memorial to the destruction of Rotterdam in World War II. You can see a miniature of this piece, **"Torso of the Ruined Town,"** in the cottage's pleasant garden, along with the rest of the museum's larger works. Gallery Two holds a selection of his cubist sculptures, such as **"Woman and Fan"** in bronze and **"Beautiful Servant Girl"** in stone. Gallery Four is dedicated to works in wood—a medium that Zadkine was particularly interested in—and includes sculpture from throughout his career. The museum also hosts exhibitions from guest artists.

100 rue d'Assas, 6th arr. • 01 55 42 77 20 • Closed Mon. and public holidays • Métro: Vavin

Cimetière du Montparnasse

7 In 1824, three farms were combined to form what became one of Paris's most famous cemeteries. The 47-acre (19 ha) burial ground is the final resting place for more than 300,000 people, including many of the area's luminaries. Just inside the entrance, where you can pick up a free map, are the **joint plots** of the philosophers Jean-Paul Sartre and his companion Simone de Beauvoir. Wander around the cemetery's garden-like setting, with

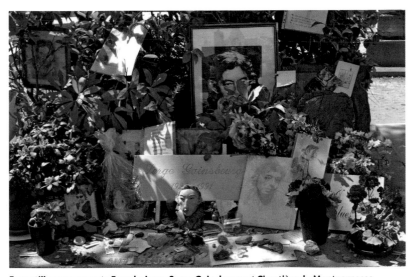

Fans still commemorate French singer Serge Gainsbourg at Cimetière du Montparnasse.

wide, paved walkways, fountains, and sculptures, to stumble across **tombs** of well-known people, such as poet Charles Baudelaire, author Susan Sontag, and Irish playwright Samuel Beckett.

3 blvd. Edgar Quinet, 14th arr. • 01 44 10 86 50 • Métro: Edgar Quinet or Raspail

Tour Montparnasse

8 Towering 690 feet (210 m) above the ground, this often-criticized building opened in 1973 and dwarfs everything else in the district. The 56th floor remains the main attraction, with a spectacular 360-degree view that extends up to 40 miles (64 km) on a clear day. The floor has displays of the city's monuments, a 15-minute film, photo exhibits, a gift shop, bar, café, and a gourmet restaurant, Le Ciel de Paris *(01 40 64 77 64, reservation only, €€€€)*.

33 ave. du Maine, 15th arr. • www.tourmontparnasse56.com • 01 45 38 52 56
• Elevator to 56th floor: €€ • Métro: Montparnasse-Bienvenüe

Parks & Gardens

Parisian gardens were a sign of riches and power for the royal, wealthy, and noble, who created idyllic landscapes as a backdrop for elaborate parties, entertainments, and theatrical events. Over the centuries, French gardens took many forms according to the fashions of the times. The formal garden, however, was the most influential and enduring style—it is what we think of as the quintessential French garden.

You can rent model sailboats (above) in several of Paris's gardens. The Jardin du Luxembourg (right) is a popular place to rest in the summer sun.

Royal Gardens

Italian Renaissance gardens, inspired by classical ideals of beauty and order, were a heavy influence on *jardins à la française*. Queen Catherine de Médicis, the Italian wife of King Henri II, built one of Paris's oldest gardens, the **Jardin des Tuileries** (see pp. 118–119), in 1564, in an Italian style. In the 17th-century, landscape designer André Le Nôtre redrew the garden in its present form. He was a master of French formal gardens and his geometric shapes and symmetrical patterns aimed to show man's control over nature, and thus the power and prestige of the garden's owner.

The **Jardin du Luxembourg** (see pp. 75–76) was created in 1612 by another Italian, Queen Marie de Médicis, to remind her of the gardens of her youth. In the 19th century, architect Jean-François-Thérèse Chalgrin restored the gardens, which are composed of several parts—a formal garden, an "English" garden, a woody area, lawns, and an orchard—all crossed by paths that beckon visitors to take a relaxing stroll.

Second Empire Legacy

Today's Parisian gardens owe their appearance to Second Empire fashion. After the French Revolution, formal gardens with their strict, symmetrical forms were discarded in favor of an English style that re-created an idyllic pastoral landscape, complete with lakes, bridges, ruins, and temples—such as **Parc Monceau** (see p. 136). At the same time, the creation of green space became necessary to provide the city's population with some fresh air. Nineteenth-century city planner Baron Haussmann created the **Bois de Boulogne** and the **Bois de Vincennes,** which were landscaped with open lawns and woodlands; these immense parks still constitute the city's largest green spaces.

MODERN **PARKS**

André Citroën Park
Opened in 1992, this park on the former site of the Citroën factory comprises a central lawn around fountains, greenhouses, a canal, and small gardens.
Quai André Citröen, 15th arr., www.gardenvisit.com

Parc de la Villette Built in the 1980s, this large park is filled with modernist architectural follies, as well as plenty of green space. It is also home to themed gardens such as a garden of mirrors and a bamboo forest, and a science museum (see p. 35). **Ave. Jean Jaurés, 19th arr., www.garden visit.com**

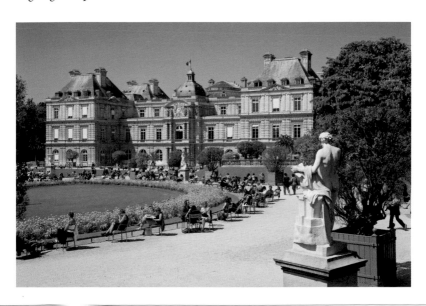

Small Museums

Paris may be renowned for colossal collections such as the Louvre, but the French capital also boasts an array of great small museums. Visit humble accumulations of art, including the homes of artists, writers, and singers, and a homage to wine.

■ MUSÉE BOURDELLE

Sculpture and other art fills the Montparnasse home, garden, and workshop of 19th-century artist Antoine Bourdelle—a protégé of Auguste Rodin. From 21 dramatic **busts of Beethoven** to figures from Greek mythology and sensuous **female nudes,** the collection reflects Bourdelle's range. The museum also houses art from Rodin, Eugène Delacroix, and other artists.

18 rue Antoine Bourdelle, 15th arr. • 01 49 54 73 73 • Closed Mon. and public holidays • €€

■ MAISON DE VICTOR HUGO

France's preeminent writer drew more than two million people to his funeral at St.-Sulpice in 1885, demonstrating the nation's affection for the author of *Les Misérables* and *The Hunchback of Notre Dame.* Victor Hugo wrote many of his works on the second floor of this former hotel in Le Marais, where

he lived from 1832 to 1848. The reconstructed rooms display photos, furniture, documents, and other mementos from his life, including 450 of his sketches and drawings.

6 place des Vosges, 4th arr. • 01 42 72 10 16 • Closed Mon. and public holidays

■ MUSÉE ÉDITH PIAF

France's greatest singer was born Edith Giovanna Gassion in 1915. By her mid-30s, the celebrated chanteuse had risen to musical fame both at home and abroad with hits such as *"Non, Je ne Regrette Rien"* and *"La Vie en Rose."* This apartment (close to where she grew up in Belleville), north of Le Marais, houses a private memorial to the singer, with photos, jewelry, outfits, music memorabilia, and other personal effects from her life. Call ahead for a key code to access the museum.

5 rue Crespin du Gast, 11th arr. • 01 43 55 52 72 • Closed Fri., Sat., Sun., and public holidays

Musée Édith Piaf is the personal collection of Bernard Marchois, a lifelong fan of the singer.

■ Musée du Vin

The medieval stone-walled cellars of a 15th-century monastery close to the Jardins du Trocadéro house the museum of the Conseil des Échansons de France, a group devoted to fine French wine. Displays, waxwork figures, and artifacts such as wine bottles, vats, corkscrews, glasses, and decanters demonstrate winemaking and viticulture techniques throughout the ages. There's a restaurant and a shop, and you can also enjoy a wine-tasting session delivered by an expert.

5/7 square Charles Dickens, 16th arr. • 01 45 25 63 26 • Closed Mon., Jan. 1, and Dec. 25–31

■ Musée Marmottan– Claude Monet

Art historian Paul Marmottan bequeathed his house on the edge of Bois de Boulogne, together with his extensive collection of Renaissance, Consular, and First Empire art, to the Institut de France in 1932. The collection was expanded in 1966, when Impressionist Claude Monet's son donated 65 of his father's works, including several **Water Lilies** and **"Impression—Sunrise"** from the Rouen Cathedral Series.

2 rue Louis Boilly, 16th arr. • 01 40 50 65 84 • Closed Mon., Jan. 1, May 1, and Dec. 25

Châtelet &
Les Halles

For more than 800 years, the neighborhood of Les Halles held Paris's central food market. Today, the area is dominated by the Forum des Halles shopping mall, which is undergoing renovations until 2016. Yet there are still enough butchers, small markets, and food shops in the side streets to feel like you're in "the belly of Paris" during its heyday. To the east, some of the city's oldest streets surround the modernistic Centre Pompidou—one of the world's leading venues for contemporary art. Head south and you'll come to the Hôtel de Ville, seat of the city government since the 14th century and once the site of Paris's main port. Place du Châtelet marks the location of a long-gone fortress that once guarded a gate into the city. The whole area contains a treasury of monuments.

◗ **Église St.-Eustache has served some notable parishioners, including Cardinal Richelieu, Mozart, and Madame de Pompadour.**

Châtelet & Les Halles

The area around Paris's former central market has one of the world's best museums of contemporary art and many historic squares and streets.

1 Église St.-Eustache (see p. 86) Start at the Church of St.-Eustache, an unfinished masterpiece of Gothic architecture. Head east on rue Rambuteau, and turn south on rue Pierrre Lescot.

2 Forum & Jardin des Halles (see pp. 86–87) The former site of the central food market is a large public garden above an underground shopping mall. The mall is open, but renovation work on the garden will continue until 2016.

3 Fontaine des Innocents (see p. 87) This beautiful nymph-adorned, Renaissance-style fountain sits in the Place Joachim du Bellay. Continue on rue Berger, cross boulevard de Sébastopol, and walk two blocks to Place Georges Pompidou.

4 Centre Pompidou (see pp. 90–91) This cultural center is home to the Musée National d'Art Moderne, and the building is an attraction in itself. Head east on rue Aubry le Boucher, turn right on rue du Renard, and left on rue de Rivoli, to reach Place de l'Hôtel de Ville.

Map labels: Sentier (M), RUE D'ABOUKIR, RUE, RUE MONTMARTRE, RUE ÉTIENNE MARCEL, RUE DU LOUVRE, Église St.-Eustache, Étienne Marc (M), **1**, Les Halles (M), JARDIN DES HALLES, Forum & Jardin des Halles **2**, RUE ST.-HONORÉ, **3** Fontaine des Innocents, RUE DE RIVOLI, RUE DU PONT NEUF, RUE DES HALLES, BOULEVA, Pont Neuf (M), Seine, RUE DE RIVOLI, Châtelet (M), Place du Châtelet **6**, AVE VICTOR, QUAI DE GESVRE, PONT AU CHANGE, PONT NOTRE-DAME

**CHÂTELET & LES HALLES DISTANCE: 1 MILE (1.6 KM)
TIME: APPROX. 4 HOURS MÉTRO START: LES HALLES**

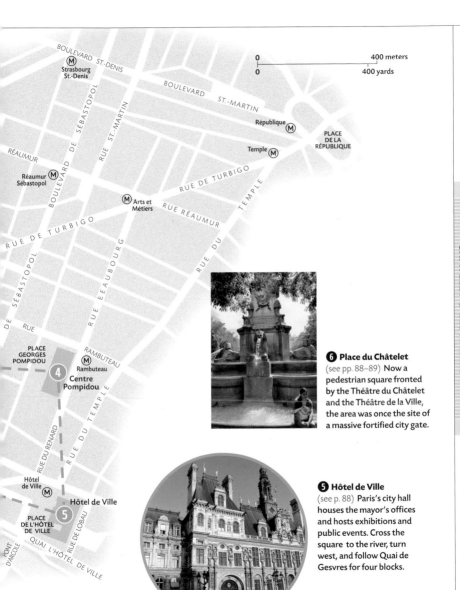

0
400 meters

0
400 yards

BOULEVARD ST-DENIS

Ⓜ Strasbourg St.-Denis

BOULEVARD ST.-MARTIN

Ⓜ République

PLACE DE LA RÉPUBLIQUE

Ⓜ Temple

RUE ST.-MARTIN

BOULEVARD DE SÉBASTOPOL

RÉAUMUR

Ⓜ Réaumur Sébastopol

Ⓜ Arts et Métiers

RUE DE TURBIGO

RUE RÉAUMUR

RUE DU TEMPLE

RUE DE TURBIGO

RUE DE SÉBASTOPOL

RUE BEAUBOURG

DE RUE

PLACE GEORGES POMPIDOU

RAMBUTEAU

Ⓜ Rambuteau

④ Centre Pompidou

RUE DU TEMPLE

RUE DU RENARD

Hôtel de Ville Ⓜ

Hôtel de Ville

PLACE DE L'HÔTEL DE VILLE

⑤

RUE DE LOBAU

QUAI L'HÔTEL DE VILLE

PONT D'ARCOLE

CHÂTELET & LES HALLES

❻ Place du Châtelet
(see pp. 88–89) Now a pedestrian square fronted by the Théâtre du Châtelet and the Théâtre de la Ville, the area was once the site of a massive fortified city gate.

❺ Hôtel de Ville
(see p. 88) Paris's city hall houses the mayor's offices and hosts exhibitions and public events. Cross the square to the river, turn west, and follow Quai de Gesvres for four blocks.

NEIGHBORHOOD WALK | **85**

Église St.-Eustache

1 The first church to occupy this site was founded in 1223 by a local resident named Jean Alaias. Alaias had loaned King Philippe-Auguste a substantial sum; as repayment, the king authorized him to take a percentage from every bushel of fish sold at the neighboring market, and Alaias used his resulting fortune to build a chapel. Construction of the current church began in 1532 and took more than a hundred years. The structure is Gothic, with flying buttresses on the exterior and ribbed vaulting in the nave, but arches, columns, and pillars from the Renaissance fill the interior. Like many of Paris's churches, St.-Eustache was pillaged during the revolution and subsequently used as a barn. Now restored, its interior includes **stained-glass windows** created by Antoine Soulignac in 1632, several paintings by Peter Paul Rubens, including the **"Emmaus Pilgrims,"** and a modern sculpture by Raymond Mason, **"The Departure of Fruit and Vegetables from the Heart of Paris on the 28th February 1969,"** in one of the side chapels. The church has a strong musical tradition—Liszt and Berlioz performed here—and, with 8,000 pipes, the **Van den Heuvel organ** is among Paris's largest.

2 impasse St.-Eustache, 1st arr. • 01 42 36 31 05 • Métro: Châtelet or Étienne Marcel

Forum & Jardin des Halles

2 Paris's central market stood in Les Halles between the 12th century and 1969. The market began in the open, but in 1181, King Philippe-Auguste built two halls to shelter textile makers, and in 1543 King François I had additional buildings constructed in order to improve the market's hygiene. Sanitation problems continued to plague the area until the 1850s, when Napoleon III ordered improvements be made, including the construction of cast-iron-and-glass pavilions designed by architect Victor Baltard. The market moved to Rungis, south of Paris, in 1969, and Baltard's pavilions were demolished. The only architectural remnant of the old market is the **Bourse du Commerce,** the rotunda at the western end of the gardens that once served as a grain market. The present **Forum des Halles,** built in 1979, is a subterranean shopping center topped by **public gardens** with tree-lined walkways, lawns, a tropical greenhouse, and a children's garden. Despite being popular with suburban youth, the shopping mall has declined in fortunes over the years. Les Halles is currently undergoing another massive modernization, scheduled for completion in 2016.

Rue des Halles, off rue de Rivoli, 1st arr. • Métro: Châtelet

Fontaine des Innocents

3 Paris's only Renaissance fountain was built in 1549 to commemorate King Henri II's first entry into the city. Originally positioned against the wall of the Cimetière des Sts.-Innocents (Cemetery of the Holy Innocents), on the corner of rue Berger and rue St.-Denis, notables used it as a viewing platform to watch Henri's procession. This enormous fountain was designed by Palais du Louvre architect Pierre Lescot (see pp. 122–125) and decorated by sculptor Jean Goujon in the style of a Roman triumphal arch, with **relief carvings** of *putti* (cherubs) and veiled nymphs pouring water between Corinthian columns. In 1810, the bas-reliefs around the base were removed to the Louvre so they would not be eroded by the water flowing over them from the large brass font.

Place Joachim du Bellay, rue St.-Denis, 1st arr. • Métro: Châtelet

Centre Pompidou

4 See pp. 90–91.

Place Georges Pompidou, 4th arr. • www.centre pompidou.fr • 01 44 78 12 33 • Musée National d'Art Moderne: €€€, access to level 6 walkway: € • Closed Tues. and May 1 • Métro: Rambuteau or Châtelet

Water gushes down the stepped pedestal of the Fontaine des Innocents, decorated with angels and nymphs.

Hôtel de Ville

5 Paris's city hall has played a central role in civic life since the 11th century, as a center of commerce, government, public demonstrations, and no small number of executions. In 1264, under the auspices of King Louis IX, merchants elected the city's first municipal authority figures. In 1357, provost Étienne Marcel bought a mansion by the Seine to use for meetings, and since then the city government has been located on this spot. During the 1871 uprising the current building, dating from 1628, was consumed by fire. The hall's present appearance—ornately decorated with turrets and detailed stonework—dates from the heavy restoration that took place from 1874 to 1882. The facade is adorned with thirty statues representing French towns and 108 statues of famous people born in Paris. An allegorical figure representing Paris sits above the clock. Inside are the mayor's offices and exhibition spaces.

Until 1830, the **Place de l'Hôtel de Ville** was called the Place de Grève. *Grève* means "beach," or "strand," and traders and merchants used this spot as a riverside port to bring their goods in to the city. The expression *faire la grève,* meaning "to go on strike," originated here, where unhappy workers gathered to protest. Today the square is used for concerts, festivals, and other events.

29 rue de Rivoli, 4th arr. • www.paris.fr • 01 42 76 40 40
• Group visits only: reservations required, 01 42 76 54 04
• Métro: Hôtel de Ville

GOOD **EATS**

■ **LA RÉGALADE ST.-HONORÉ**
This second location of the classic La Régalade, near the Jardin des Halles, serves up seasonal bistro cooking from chef Bruno Doucet. **123 rue St.-Honoré, 1st arr., 01 42 21 92 40, €€**

■ **SPRING**
American chef Daniel Rose lets the market—and his whim—dictate the six-course menu he offers each evening near Les Halles. **6 rue Bailleul, 1st arr., 01 45 96 05 72, €€€€**

■ **LA TOUR DE MONTLHÉRY (CHEZ DENISE)**
The old food market lives on at this classic, meat-heavy restaurant to the east of the Forum des Halles. **5 rue des Prouvaires, 1st arr., 01 42 36 21 82, €€€**

Place du Châtelet

6 This pedestrianized square is named for the Grand Châtelet, a 12th-century fortified city gate that protected the Île de la Cité and later housed courts, police offices, and a prison that was

A temporary sculpture installation fills the Place de l'Hôtel de Ville.

even more feared for its unpleasant conditions than the nearby Bastille. Napoleon destroyed the fort in 1808 and created the present-day square. At the center is the **Fontaine du Palmier** (Palmier Fountain), topped by a column erected in 1808 to honor Napoleon's victories in Egypt and Italy. Facing onto the square are two Haussmann-era theaters, **Théâtre de la Ville** *(2 place du Châtelet, 4th arr., www.theatredelaville-paris.com, 01 42 74 22 77)* and **Théâtre du Châtelet** *(1 place du Châtelet, 1st arr., www.chatelet-theatre.com, 01 40 28 28 40)*, designed by architect Jean-Antoine-Gabriel Davioud and built in the early 1860s. The neighboring garden focuses on the **Tour St.-Jacques,** a Gothic tower from a church that was destroyed following the French Revolution. Pilgrims used the church, built by the butchers' guild, as a meeting point on their way to Santiago de Compostela in Spain.

Quai de la Mégisserie/blvd. de Sébastopol, 1st and 4th arr. • Métro: Châtelet

Centre Pompidou

The Centre Pompidou is a cultural institution showcasing modern and contemporary visual arts, music, performance, and film.

With so much on the outside (such as escalators), Centre Pompidou has more room for art.

Designed by architects Renzo Piano and Richard Rogers in 1977, the building housing the Centre Pompidou wears its inner workings—electricity, water, and air—on the outside in a primary-color maze of pipes and ducts. The popular Public Information Library occupies the first three levels, but the main attraction is the Musée National d'Art Moderne (the National Museum of Modern Art), a world-class collection of visual and multimedia works from 1905 to the present on Levels 4 and 5, plus changing exhibitions on Level 6.

■ Art of Today

On Level 4, the contemporary collection features works from 1960 to the present and is updated every two years to remain truly current. The Central Gallery provides a chronological tour through arte povera, pop art, minimalism, and other contemporary movements. Watch for Andy Warhol's prints of Elizabeth Taylor called **"Ten Lizes,"** Cy Twombly's sculpture **"Untitled,"** and Carsten Höller's three-dimensional **"Giant Triple Mushroom."** Design, architecture, photography, and multimedia installations mingle in a series of spacious side rooms. Don't miss the **Agam Salon,** a polychromatic, kinetic space by Yaacov Agam that President Georges Pompidou commissioned in 1974 for his private quarters at the Élysée Palace.

■ The 20th-century View

Level 5 showcases works created between 1905 and 1960. Beginning with the fauves, the exhibits move through a timeline of 20th-century art—cubism, expressionism, surrealism, and abstraction. Highlights include pioneering works of cubism such as

Georges Braque's **"Viaduct at Estaque"** and Pablo Picasso's **"The Guitarist"** (Room 4), surrealist masterpiece **"The Bather"** by Joan Miró (Room 14), and a grand swath of paintings by Henri Matisse, including **"Violinist at the Window"** and **"The Open Window at Collioure"** (Room 3).

■ Dine on Set

The chic **Restaurant Georges** (*01 44 78 47 99, €€€–€€€€*) on Level 6 is often likened to a Stanley Kubrick film set.

■ Place Georges Pompidou

The **Atelier Brancusi** is a time capsule of the sculptor Constantin Brancusi's studio, more or less as he left it when he died in 1957. Four sections of his studio have been re-created and include finished works as well as models, sketches, tools, and furniture. The square itself hosts outdoor art installations and some of Paris's best performance art and street theater.

Place Georges Pompidou, 4th arr. • www.centrepompidou.fr • 01 44 78 12 33 • €€€ (first Sun. of the month free) • Closed Tues. and May 1; Atelier Brancusi: closed a.m. • Métro: Rambuteau or Châtelet

CHÂTELET & LES HALLES

Culinary Capital

The French love their food. Indeed, the restaurant, derived from the French word *restaurer* (to restore), is believed to have originated in Paris in 1765 with Monsieur Boulanger, who served a selection of pig's-and-sheep's-foot broths to workers in Les Halles. Soon establishments devoted entirely to eating were springing up all over the city, including Café de Chartres (renamed Le Grand Véfour; see p. 121), which has served fine food to the city's elite for more than 200 years.

CHÂTELET & LES HALLES

A chocolate and grapefruit dessert (above) at Le Grand Véfour (see p. 121); shoppers browse in E. Dehillerin (right), founded in 1820 and one of Paris's top specialist cookware shops.

Luxury Eateries

Monsieur Boulanger's success inspired many copies. Paris's first luxury restaurant, La Grande Taverne de Londres, opened in 1782. Its owner, former royal chef Antoine Beauvilliers, was the first to combine great food with excellent service, decor, and fine wine in a public eatery. By 1804, more than 500 restaurants served Parisians.

In the late 19th century, Auguste Escoffier introduced the *Brigade de cuisine* system (influenced by his army days), which ran kitchens on a strictly hierarchical order from head chef to dishwasher—a system which is still in use today. Along with his partner, César Ritz, Escoffier opened the Hôtel Ritz, where his cooking earned him the title *Roi des Cuisiniers et Cuisinier des Rois* (King of Chefs and Chef of Kings).

Cordon Bleu

As access to fine dining increased, so did interest in cooking. In 1896, French journalist Marthe Distel founded *La Cuisinière Cordon*

Bleu culinary magazine. The name comes from a 16th-century order of knights, who wore *cordon bleus* (blue ribbons) to signify their status. To gain subscribers, Distel also offered cooking classes with some of Paris's top chefs, which soon developed into the world's first cooking school. The magazine and classes were a great success and helped to define French cuisine and spread its popularity throughout the world.

Michelin Status

In 1923, André Michelin added a star to the best restaurants in his drivers' guide book. Following World War II, the Michelin Guide spread across the world, cementing the French reputation as the experts on fine dining (See High-end Dining pp. 68–69).

PARIS **BISTROS**

The word "bistro" refers to smaller restaurants with a proprietor present—either in the kitchen or front of house—and typically serving simple food at reasonable prices, without ceremonious extras. The early 21st century saw the rise of the "neo-bistro," a movement initiated by young chefs who chose to forgo careers in Michelin-starred kitchens, instead choosing more relaxed settings to showcase their creativity and skills.

Street Markets & *Brocantes*

To experience Paris one must shop in Paris, especially at the famous *brocantes* (secondhand stalls) and *marchés aux puces* (antique flea markets). Despite its history, Les Halles is now known for its modern mall—but check out some of these markets and join your fellow Parisians as they root out a good buy.

■ RASPAIL

Conventional stalls fill this St.-Germain street on Tuesday and Friday mornings, but on Sunday mornings it is one of the city's best *biologique* (organic) food markets. The roasted free-range chicken is delicious. Also look for unusual preserves.

Blvd. Raspail between rue du Cherche Midi and rue de Rennes, 6th arr. • Open Tues., Fri., and Sun. a.m.

■ MARCHÉ AUX PUCES DE LA PORTE DE VANVES

South of Montparnasse, this market spread over two avenues offers antiques and bric-a-brac of all sorts and periods. Go early for bargains and the best pieces.

Ave. Georges Lafenestre and ave. Marc Sangnier, 14th arr. • Open Sat. and Sun. 7 a.m.–1 p.m.

■ MARCHÉ DES ENFANTS ROUGES

Named for the red-clothed children who lived at the former orphanage on this site, Paris's oldest covered market dates from the 1600s. It is more a fun place to have lunch or an early dinner in trendy Le Marais than it is a place to pick up great buys. The Japanese and Moroccan take-out stands are particularly good.

Rue de Bretagne, 3rd arr. • Closed Mon.

■ MARCHÉ DE LA BASTILLE

The Bastille area hosts the city's largest and most impressive market. Famed for its fresh food produce (the cheeses are excellent), the market is popular with Parisians because of the huge variety offered—everything from food to clothing to kitchen tools.

Blvd. Richard Lenoir between rue Amelot and rue St.-Sabin, 11th arr. • Open Sun. and Thurs. a.m.

■ MARCHÉ D'ALIGRE

Close to Place de la Bastille, this market has many colorful stalls packed with fruit and vegetables.

CHÂTELET & LES HALLES

Pick up an unusual bargain at Marché aux Puces St. Ouen de Clignancourt.

In nearby Place d'Aligre, a covered market, the **Beauvau,** sells cheeses and *charcuterie* (deli meats and pâtés). There's also a small *marché aux puces*.

Rue d'Aligre between rue de Charenton and rue du Faubourg St.-Antoine, 12th arr. • Closed Mon.

■ BATIGNOLLES

One of Paris's oldest organic markets sells fresh produce and excellent take-out food every Saturday morning. Foodies consider this Montmartre market one of the city's best places for great food.

Blvd. des Batignolles between rue des Batignolles and rue Boursault, 17th arr. • Open Sat. a.m.

■ MARCHÉ AUX PUCES ST. OUEN DE CLIGNANCOURT

One of the world's finest markets, in the north of Montmartre, has more than 2,500 shops and stalls spread over a labyrinth of alleyways, selling everything from antiques to scrap. Visit **Biron** *(No. 85)* for high-end antiques, **Serpette** *(No. 110)* for classic furniture, **Paul Bert** *(No. 96),* which sells the latest in art and collectibles, and **Vernaison** *(No. 99)*–the place to go for everything from toys to textiles.

Rue des Rosiers between ave. Michelet and rue Jean-Henri Fabre, 18th arr. • Open Sat., Sun., and Mon.

Le Marais & Bastille

One of the city's oldest and most atmospheric quarters, the area was originally marshland (*marais* means "marsh"). The Middle Ages saw swamps drained and homes erected. During the Renaissance the area came up in the world, and wealthy aristocrats built lavish mansions (*hôtels particuliers*) surrounded by high walls. Nearby was the Bastille fortress, site of the celebrated battle that began the French Revolution. Later the neighborhood went into a long decline, during which many of the grand mansions became derelict. In the 1960s, the Friends of the Marais, aware that a huge part of their architectural heritage was endangered, lobbied City Hall to refurbish the crumbling mansions. Many of the hôtels became museums, libraries, and government offices.

◐ **The narrow streets of Le Marais are lined with cafés and restaurants, where you can stop, relax, and people-watch.**

Le Marais & Bastille

From Place de la Bastille, take a stroll through Renaissance Paris via the narrow lanes and stately courtyards of the old Marais.

❹ Musée Carnavalet (see p. 102) Explore the history of Paris, then continue west along rue des Francs Bourgeois to the Musée Cognacq-Jay.

❸ Place des Vosges (see p. 101) Stop to admire what is said to be the most perfect square in Paris. Exit on the northwest side of the square, and walk two blocks down rue des Francs Bourgeois.

❷ Hôtel de Béthune-Sully (see p. 100) Stop in at this imposing 17th-century mansion's bookshop, pass through the pretty garden, and go through the doorway into the Place des Vosges.

❺ Musée Cognacq-Jay (see pp. 102–103) Admire the 18th-century collection amassed by the founders of La Samaritaine department store. Turn right out of the museum, down rue Elzévir, and left onto rue de Thorigny.

❻ Musée Picasso (see pp. 106–107) See some of the 3,000 works by the celebrated Spaniard, as well as Picasso's private collection of works by his peers Matisse, Degas, and Cézanne. Turn right out of the museum onto rue de la Perle, left onto rue Vieille du Temple, and right onto rue des Francs Bourgeois.

400 meters
400 yards

① Place de la Bastille (see p. 100) Trace the cobblestone outline of the notorious fortress prison where the French Revolution started. Exit on the western edge of the circle, and move down rue St.-Antoine.

⑦ Archives Nationales (see p. 103) Rotating exhibits feature priceless documents and artifacts from France's long and glorious past. Head west along rue Rambuteau and turn right onto rue du Temple.

⑧ Musée d'Art et d'Histoire du Judaïsme (see p. 104) Jewish art, culture, and history are the focus of this dynamic small museum. Retrace your steps along rue des Francs Bourgeois, turn right onto rue Vieille du Temple, and left on rue des Rosiers.

⑨ The Pletzl (see pp. 104–105) Explore Paris's Jewish quarter in this warren of streets, especially along rue des Rosiers. Follow rue Pavée south, cross rue de Rivoli onto rue de Fourcy, and go left on rue de l'Hôtel de Ville.

⑩ Hôtel de Sens (see p. 105) Now an arts library, this imposing mansion blends Gothic and Renaissance architecture. The back garden provides a great place to relax at the end of your Marais walk.

LE MARAIS & BASTILLE DISTANCE: APPROX 2.1 MILES (3.5 KM) TIME: APPROX. 6–8 HOURS METRO START: BASTILLE

LE MARAIS & BASTILLE

Place de la Bastille

1 The French Revolution went from mere talk to bloody combat when an angry mob stormed the Bastille, a fortified prison and armory, on the afternoon of July 14, 1789. Four hours later the Bastille had fallen, the prisoners held inside were free, and the monarchy was on the verge of collapse. The bastion's former boundaries are traced in cobblestones outside Nos. 5–49 boulevard Henri IV. The **Colonne de Juillet** (July Column)—topped by the golden **Génie de la Liberté** (Spirit of Liberty)—commemorates both the 1789 rebellion and a later uprising in 1830. The strikingly modern curved glass facade of the **Opéra de la Bastille** *(120 rue de Lyon, 4th arr., www.operadeparis.fr, 01 43 47 13 22, tours €€€)*, home of the Opéra National de Paris, looms on the southeastern side of the square. The 2,700-seat theater, designed by Carlos Ott, was opened in 1989 to mark the bicentennial of the revolution. Guided tours include the main auditorium and the backstage areas.

At the end of rue St.-Antoine, 3rd/4th/11th arr. • Métro: Bastille

Hôtel de Béthune-Sully

2 Built in the early 17th century as a private home and later owned by Maximilien de Béthune, the Duke of Sully, finance minister to King Henri IV, the mansion is one of the city's best examples of King Louis XIII architecture. Now home to the **Centre des Monuments Nationaux** (the National Office for Historical Monuments), caretaker of France's national treasures, it features a photography gallery that hosts temporary exhibits, a bookshop, and a garden. The bookshop has a **17th-century ceiling** with painted beams and window embrasures. From the outer courtyard, decorated with guardian sphinxes and figures representing the seasons and elements, you pass through a porch into the rear garden, which provides a handy shortcut to the Place des Vosges.

62 rue St.-Antoine, 4th arr. • www.sully.monuments-nationaux.fr • 01 44 61 21 50
• Métro: Bastille or Sully Morland

Place des Vosges

3 The early 17th-century town-house mansions that surround the square are noted for their elegant brick facades and long arcades that front trendy restaurants, cafés, boutiques, and art galleries. Built between 1605 and 1612 at the behest of King Henri IV, the square was one of Europe's first attempts at modern city planning and became a template for later developments across the continent. Originally called the Place Royale, although no kings or queens ever lived here, the name was changed during the revolution to honor France's eastern Vosges region: the first to contribute taxes to the new government. Cardinal Richelieu lived at **No. 21** from 1615 to 1627, but the square's most celebrated habitué was the author Victor Hugo. He moved into **No. 6** in the early 1830s, shortly after his novel *Notre-Dame de Paris (The Hunchback of Notre-Dame)* became a best seller. His former home is now a museum (see p. 80).

Off rue des Francs Bourgeois, 4th arr. • Métro: Bastille, St.-Paul, or Chemin Vert

Place des Vosges is perfectly symmetrical, with nine houses on each of its four sides.

Among the Musée Carnavalet's displays is the re-creation of a room from one of the royal palaces in the reign of Louis XVI.

Musée Carnavalet

4 An ancient recipe for frog's leg soup and Robespierre's farewell letter before facing the guillotine are among the oddities found inside the official historical museum of the city of Paris. The collection is arranged chronologically and sprawls through more than a hundred galleries in two adjacent buildings, the Hôtel Carnavalet and Hôtel Le Peletier de St. Fargeau. The former is a splendid Renaissance mansion, completed in 1548 and later the home of aristocratic letter-writer Marie de Rabutin-Chantal (Madame de Sévigné). A comprehensive look at the city's cultural, intellectual, and spiritual life, the museum covers more than 2,000 years of Parisian history—from the Gauls and Romans through modern times—and ranges from a prehistoric dugout canoe once used on the Seine to the personal effects of Marie-Antoinette. Don't miss the **Sign Galleries,** an unusual collection of street signage from the 16th through 20th centuries; the reassembled study from the 17th-century Hôtel La Rivière and reception room from the Hôtel d'Uzès; **a scale model of the Bastille;** and various artifacts from the French Revolution including an ornately decorated copy of **The Declaration of the Rights of Man.**

23 rue de Sévigné, 3rd arr. • www.carnavalet.paris.fr • 01 44 59 58 58 • Closed Mon. • Métro: St.-Paul, Chemin Vert, or Bastille

Musée Cognacq-Jay

5 Ernest Cognacq (1839–1928), founder of La Samaritaine department store, began life as a lowly necktie vendor on the Pont Neuf. Even more than his emporium, the museum in his former home shows just how far he climbed during his lifetime. The vast array of paintings, sculptures, jewelry, furniture, and ceramics was amassed by Cognacq and his wife, Marie-Louise Jay, who shared his passion for fine art. The emphasis is on 18th-century France,

LE MARAIS & BASTILLE

displayed in the likeminded surroundings of the Hôtel Donon with its exquisite **Louis XV and XVI rooms.** The eclectic collection also contains paintings by Rembrandt, as well as works by Impressionists Paul Cézanne and Edgar Degas. Head up to the attic to see the **exposed roof beams** that let you see how the building was constructed.

8 rue Elzévir, 3rd arr. • http://en.parisinfo.com/museum-monuments/237/musee-cognacq-jay • 01 40 27 07 21 • Closed Mon. and public holidays • Métro: St.-Paul, Chemin Vert, or Rambuteau

Musée Picasso

6 See pp. 106–107.

Hôtel Salé, 5 rue de Thorigny, 3rd arr. • www.musee-picasso.fr • 01 42 71 25 21 • Closed for renovation until 2013 • Métro: St.-Sébastien-Froissart or Chemin Vert

Archives Nationales

7 France's National Archives—one of the few institutions created rather than destroyed during the revolution—are housed in several adjacent 17th-century mansions. Most impressive of these is the **Palais Soubise,** named for the noblewoman and onetime mistress of King Louis XIV who remodeled it (allegedly with the Sun King's funds) into one of the most dazzling residences in the Marais—her apartments show how the nobility lived before the revolution. The archive's treasures are displayed in revolving exhibits in the **Musée de l'Histoire de France.** Among the artifacts are the jailer's keys from the Bastille, the only known portrait of Joan of Arc rendered during her lifetime, the **Edict of Nantes** (1598) that granted Protestants the right to worship in France, **Louis XVI's will,** and Marie-Antoinette's farewell letter.

63 rue des Francs Bourgeois, 3rd arr. • 01 40 27 60 96 • € • Closed Tues. • Métro: Rambuteau or Hôtel de Ville

LE MARAIS & BASTILLE

Musée d'Art et d'Histoire du Judaïsme

8 The permanent collection runs a broad gamut from ancient Torah scrolls and Hanukkah lamps to modern artworks by Jewish artists from Europe and the Middle East, covering both the Ashkenazi and Sephardic worlds. It also takes in Jewish intellectual and political movements, the diaspora, and Jewish culture during the Middle Ages and Renaissance. The collection is housed in the meticulously restored **Hôtel de St.-Aignan,** built as the city residence of the Count d'Avaux. By the mid 19th-century, the mansion had been subdivided into numerous units, many of them occupied by émigré Jews from Eastern Europe. Among the building's most intriguing features are the rebuilt **grand staircase** and the **dining room** with its recently rediscovered Roman-style grisaille wall decorations.

71 rue du Temple, 3rd arr. • www.mahj.org • 01 53 01 86 53 • €€ • Closed Sat. • Métro: Rambuteau or Hôtel de Ville

The Pletzl

9 As early as the 13th century, Jews began to congregate in the Marais after they were expelled from the main city. Immigrants from Eastern Europe and Russia arrived during the 19th and early 20th centuries. Despite nearly five years of Nazi occupation and the loss of more than half the population in concentration camps, the neighborhood somehow survived. The name means "little place" in Yiddish, a fitting appellation for the warren of narrow streets that compose today's Jewish quarter. **Rue des Rosiers** is the main thoroughfare, so called because roses were planted here in the Middle Ages. Kosher restaurants and food shops are among the Pletzl's trademarks. The art nouveau-style Orthodox

GOOD **EATS**

■ **L'AS DU FALLAFEL**
Order this famous Pletzl kebab house's falafel special, which brims with hummus, fried eggplant, and other tasty ingredients, and eat it in the street, like the locals do. There is a sit-down section as well. **34 rue des Rosiers, 4th arr., 01 48 87 63 60, €**

■ **MA BOURGOGNE**
Perch at a sidewalk table on the Place des Vosges for rich Burgundy-style cuisine and wines. Specialties include Beaujolais sausages, steak tartare, and lamb chops, as well as breakfast. **9 place des Vosges, 4th arr., 01 42 78 44 64, €€€**

■ **LE TRUMILOU**
Enjoy views of Notre-Dame and the Panthéon on the other side of the Seine at this neighborhood brasserie, bar, and café as you tuck into the fixed-price menu. **84 quai de l'Hôtel-de-Ville, 4th arr., 01 42 77 63 98, €€**

LE MARAIS & BASTILLE

Kosher bakeries, charcuteries, and other specialist food outlets fill rue des Rosiers in the Marais.

synagogue **Agudath Hakehilot** *(10 rue Pavée)* was designed by Hector Guimard, creator of the wrought-iron entrances of the métro. Dynamited by the Nazis in 1940, it has now been restored.

Rue des Rosiers, rue Pavée, and rue des Écouffes, 4th arr. • Métro: St.-Paul

Hôtel de Sens

10 Created between 1475 and 1507 and one of the few remaining examples of Gothic domestic architecture in Paris, the Hôtel de Sens was originally the lavish pied-à-terre of the archbishops of Sens. Later residents included the scandalous Queen Margot (wife of King Henri IV) and her many lovers. Nowadays the Hôtel de Sens houses an arts library, the **Bibliothèque Forney,** including a collection of historic posters, photos, and postcards.

1 rue Figuier, 4th arr. • 01 42 78 14 60 • € • Closed Sun. and Mon. • Métro: Pont Marie or Sully Morland

Musée Picasso

This collection, the world's largest gathering of works by Pablo Picasso, shows what he achieved in decades of artistic innovation.

Picasso's cubist work, "Still Life with Chair-Caning" (1912), combines paint and collage.

Picasso (1881–1973) once said, "Give me a museum and I'll fill it," and the Musée Picasso shows that he could. Located in a grand 17th-century mansion in the Marais, the Musée Picasso is filled with pieces that were inherited from the artist's estate in lieu of inheritance tax. The museum, small enough to tour in two hours, is arranged chronologically and provides a distilled and fascinating narrative about the development of modern art through the work of its pioneering Spanish genius.

PORTRAITS

"Head of a Dead Casagemas" (1901)—painted when Picasso was just 20 years old—is a powerful depiction of his friend Casagemas, who had committed suicide. In **"Celestina"** (1904), a harrowing oil portrait painted during the artist's somber Blue Period, a worn yet tough-looking woman stares through the viewer with her one functioning eye. Returning to naturalism, the striking but unfinished **"Portrait of Olga in an Armchair"** (1917) reminds the viewer that Picasso knew and understood the rules of European art before inverting, exploding, and reinventing them.

CUBISM

One of the major movements of modern art, cubism tackles the paradox of painting—that one depicts three-dimensional subjects on a two-dimensional surface—head on. The cubist response to this dilemma is to deconstruct subjects and reassemble the component cubes into a single abstract work. **"Le Sacré-Coeur"** (1909–1910) is a delicate composition in white and a relatively early experiment in cubism. The later **"Still Life with Chair-Caning"** (1912) integrates rope, chair caning, words, and painted cubist passages. This small work is a landmark in Picasso's career and modern art in general. It is one of the first works to combine painting and "found objects," everyday things co-opted into art.

SCULPTURE

The hefty bronze bust of the artist's lover, **"The Head of Fernande"** (1909), has cubist elements. **"Mandolin and Clarinet"** is a quirky melding of instruments. Here, Picasso continues to show his versatility and skill by reinterpreting one of his favorite subjects—musical instruments—in firewood. The sculpture demonstrates the charming caprice and flight of fancy that runs throughout Picasso's oeuvre.

IN THE KNOW

The Musée Picasso closed for renovation in 2009 and will reopen in 2013. Celebrity architect Jean-François Bodin—who has worked on many French museums, including Paris's Centre Pompidou—is directing the project. Just like the work it will house, the redesigned space promises to be interesting and innovative.

LE MARAIS & BASTILLE

Hôtel Salé, 5 rue de Thorigny, 3rd arr. • www.musee-picasso.fr • 01 42 71 25 21 • Closed for renovation until 2013 • Métro: St.-Sébastien-Froissart or Chemin Vert

Revolutionary Paris

A bankrupt government, food shortages, and discontent among the masses set the stage for revolution; its flashpoint came at the storming of the Bastille on July 14, 1789. From here you can trace the course of the revolution—from the site of the Palais des Tuileries to the Conciergerie, where Queen Marie-Antoinette was imprisoned after King Louis XVI's execution, and on to the place where Madame Guillotine performed her bloody work.

THE GUILLOTINE.

The guillotine (above) was a grimly efficient method of execution. The painter of this view of the storming of the Bastille (right) owned a nearby wine shop and painted what he saw that day.

An Unpopular King and a Popular Uprising

In May 1789, King Louis XVI convened the Estates-General (an advisory body of nobles, church leaders, and citizens) in response to growing public unrest. The citizen leaders formed the National Assembly and pledged not to disband until France had a constitution that guaranteed the rights of ordinary people. The king tried to regain control by banning the Assembly, summoning troops to Paris, and dismissing the popular finance minister, Jacques Necker, on July 11. Three days later, a crowd attacked the Bastille, the king's prison and a symbol of royal authority, looking for weapons and ammunition.

The Fall of the Monarchy

In October 1789, the revolutionaries moved the royal family from Versailles to the Palais des Tuileries (see p. 118–119). By the summer of 1792, the Paris Commune (which had governed the city since the storming of the Bastille) gained the upper hand over more moderate factions, and from the **Hôtel de**

Ville (see p. 88) revolutionary leaders Danton, Marat, and Robespierre plotted the final, bloody steps—the arrest of the royal family, who were moved to the Temple prison (later dismantled). In 1793, Louis XVI and Marie-Antoinette were executed in **Place de la Concorde** (see p. 134), along with 2,000 opponents of the revolution.

The Reign of Terror

In fall 1793, the ten-month Reign of Terror began. As many as 40,000 people may have perished. Having dispensed with their enemies, the rebels then turned on one another. In the summer of 1794, moderates sent the last of the Commune to the guillotine, ending the revolution.

BASTILLE DAY CELEBRATIONS

Bal des Pompiers On July 13, fire stations throughout Paris host fundraising balls. Bands, drinks, and firefighters in full regalia keep revelers happy until the small hours.

Parade On July 14, troops parade down the Champs-Élysées. It's crowded so get there well before the 10 a.m. start.

Fireworks Join the crowds in front of the Tour Eiffel at 10:30 p.m. to see the fireworks display. Arrive by 8:30 p.m. to find a spot.

Signature Dishes

Start the day with a croissant and coffee as you take in the world a few bites and drops at a time. Later on, try some of the best North African cooking outside the Maghreb, or some sweet treats, or that perennial French delicacy, foie gras. End the day with *soupe à l'oignon* at one of the city's always-open brasseries.

■ VIENNOISERIE
Though these delicacies owe their name to the city of Vienna, there is nothing more Parisian than a buttery pastry. A morning in the Marais is best begun at **Au Levain du Marais** (*28 blvd. Beaumarchais, 11th arr., 01 48 05 17 14*), with a croissant whose flaky layers are impossible to count. Before climbing the Tour Eiffel, charge up with an almond version at nearby **Boulangerie Julien** (*85 rue St.-Dominique, 7th arr., 01 45 51 88 77*). Then swing through St.-Germain for a *chausson aux pommes* (apple turnover) from **Poilâne** (*8 rue du Cherche-Midi, 6th arr., 01 45 48 42 59*), which also happens to be one of Paris's best bread bakeries.

■ COUSCOUS
The cuisines of Morocco, Algeria, and Tunisia, with their *tagines* (a type of North African casserole) and *merguez* (spicy lamb sausage), are as easy to

find here as those of the other regions of France, and often come at a more reasonable price. Two wildly different couscous preparations can be found in the Latin Quarter at **Chez Hamadi** (*12 rue Boutebrie, 5th arr., 01 43 54 03 30*) and not far from Pigalle at **Wally Le Saharien** (*36 rue Rodier, 9th arr., 01 42 85 51 90*). The former provides a creamy semolina sponge to soak up the juices on top, while the latter's drier, served to the side in a fluffy mound.

■ PETITS FOURS
In elegant St.-Germain, the *macaron* (macaroon) reaches its highest expression. Those seeking a delicate meringue exterior, thin filling, and classic flavors like raspberry should visit **Ladurée** (*21 rue Bonaparte, 6th arr., 01 44 07 64 87*). For fatter, denser cookies with plenty of ganache (creamy icing) sandwiched in between, **Pierre Hermé** (*72 rue*

LE MARAIS & BASTILLE

Restorative onion soup is a Parisian classic.

Bonaparte, 6th arr., 01 43 54 47 77) is your place. From white truffle to carrot with orange and cinnamon, there is the most adventurous palette of flavors. While here, grab a rum-spiked *canelé* (Bordeaux-style baked custard) or any number of treats that Monsieur Hermé calls *Ispahan.*

■ *FOIE GRAS DE CANARD*
Restaurants high and low around Paris serve infinite variations of this liver delicacy. When the server at St.-Germain's **Chez l'Ami Jean** *(27 rue Malar, 7th arr., 01 47 05 86 89)* pulls back the lid of a cast-iron cocotte, he reveals an entire lobe of foie gras,

roasted to a lacquered, caramel-hued brown. For a more dressed-up rendition, **L'Astrance** (see p. 69) marinates the liver in *verjus* (the juice of unripe grapes) and tucks it between slices of raw mushroom on crunchy *brik* dough with hazelnut oil and a puckery lemon confit. A forkful reveals a thousand layers of taste and texture.

■ ONION SOUP
Two steps from Les Halles, at **Au Pied de Cochon** *(6 rue Coquillière, 1st arr., 01 40 13 77 00)*, the quintessential *soupe à l'oignon* is served gratinée, buried under a layer of molten cheese. Best consumed in the small hours after a night on the town.

The Louvre
& Palais-Royal

Between the north bank of the Seine and the busy rue de Rivoli, the Jardin des Tuileries and epic Musée du Louvre are Paris at its most picturesque. It is a fitting home to some of the world's most important art: Crowds flock to the Louvre for the enigmatic smile of Leonardo da Vinci's "Mona Lisa" and to the Tuileries's Orangerie to see Claude Monet's paintings of water lilies. On the north side of rue de Rivoli, clothing shops, upscale hotels, restaurants, and souvenir stores do a roaring trade. The arcaded garden of the Palais-Royal, with its mix of boutiques, antiques, and specialists in everything from music boxes to vintage couture, provides an oasis of calm. Next to the Louvre, the royal church of St.-Germain l'Auxerrois offers architectural styles from Romanesque to Gothic.

◀ The Louvre's pyramidal entrance, designed by architect I. M. Pei, was built in 1986 as commissioned by President François Mitterand.

THE LOUVRE & PALAIS-ROYAL

The Louvre & Palais-Royal

The Seine's north bank is rich in historic royal palaces and their beautiful gardens, and some of the world's most important art.

❼ Galerie Nationale du Jeu de Paume (see p. 120) This historic tennis court is now a museum of photographic and moving-image art. Walk east on rue de Rivoli, then stroll north on rue de Richelieu.

❽ Palais-Royal (and Le Grand Véfour) (see p. 121) The palace forecourt's boutiques and specialty shops are renowned. Le Grand Véfour is a historic restaurant that still serves great food.

❻ Musée de l'Orangerie (see pp. 119–120) This former palace greenhouse is home to Claude Monet's vast canvases of his lily pond and a significant collection of modern art. Walk to the garden's northwest corner.

Concorde Ⓜ

PLACE
DE LA
CONCORDE

❼

Galerie Nationale
du Jeu de Paume

RUE DE RIVOLI

Ⓜ Tuileries

Musée de
l'Orangerie

❻

Jardin des
Tuileries

❺

PORT DES TUILERIES

QUAI DES TUILERIES

PORT DES TUILERIES

Seine

PASSERELLE
LÉOPOLD-
SÉDAR-SENGHOR

PONT ROYAL

❺ Jardin des Tuileries (see pp. 118–119) Spectacular views from the Arc de Triomphe du Carrousel to the Arc de Triomphe and beyond make this a much-loved park. Walk to the southwest corner of the garden.

**THE LOUVRE & PALAIS-ROYAL   DISTANCE: 2.3 MILES (3.7 KM)
TIME: APPROX. 8 HOURS MÉTRO START: LOUVRE-RIVOLI**

❶ St.-Germain l'Auxerrois (see p. 116) This was the parish church of the royal family when the Louvre was a royal palace. Walk north on rue de l'Amiral de Coligny.

❷ Rue de Rivoli (see pp. 116–117) This busy thoroughfare was laid out on Napoleon's orders and links all the sites on this tour. Walk west.

❸ Musée des Arts Décoratifs (see p. 117) See everyday French objects from the 12th to the 20th centuries. Continue to the main entrance of the Louvre.

❹ Musée du Louvre (see pp. 122–125) A medieval fortress that was remade into a Renaissance palace, the building then became a world-class museum. Walk across Place du Carrousel to the garden.

THE LOUVRE & PALAIS-ROYAL

RUE DES PETITS CHAMPS

AVENUE DE L'OPÉRA

Ⓜ Pyramides

RUE DES PYRAMIDES

RUE ST-HONORÉ

RUE DE RICHELIEU

JARDIN DU PALAIS-ROYAL

Palais-Royal

❽

PLACE DES PYRAMIDES

PLACE A. MALRAUX

Musée de la Mode et du Textile

Comédie Française

PLACE COLETTE

PLACE DU PALAIS-ROYAL

Musée des Arts Décoratifs

❸

RUE DE RIVOLI

Palais-Royal Ⓜ Musée du Louvre

RUE ST-HONORÉ

Musée de la Publicité

JARDIN DU CARROUSEL

PLACE DU CARROUSEL

❷ Rue de Rivoli

Pyramide

❹ Musée du Louvre

RUE DE L'AMIRAL DE COLIGNY

Louvre-Rivoli Ⓜ

PORT DU LOUVRE

PONT DU CARROUSEL

JARDIN DE L'INFANTE

❶ St.-Germain l'Auxerrois

QUAI DU LOUVRE

Ⓜ Pont Neuf

Seine

0 — 400 meters
0 — 400 yards

St.-Germain l'Auxerrois

1 Many visitors to the Louvre overlook its next-door neighbor, yet this church is one of Paris's architectural highlights. When kings and queens called the Palais du Louvre home during the 14th to15th centuries, this is where they worshiped. The church, which predates the palace, was built in the 12th century, although only the foundations of the tower remain from this period. The current medieval architecture is a wondrous mix of Renaissance, Romanesque, and Gothic styles, beautifully embellished with 829 square feet (77 sq m) of **stained-glass windows** from the Renaissance. Much of the original decoration was looted during the French Revolution (when the church was used as a police station and a barn), but it was carefully restored in the 19th century. Highlights include a grand **15th-century Gothic porch** above the west doorway, an **organ** originally commissioned by King Louis XIV for the nearby Ste.-Chapelle (see p. 45), and some exquisitely carved **royal pews** based on designs by French artist Charles Le Brun. The church also has a murky past—its **bells** were rung to signal the start of the St. Bartholomew's Day Massacre (see sidebar this page).

2 place du Louvre, 1st arr. • 01 42 60 13 96 • Métro: Louvre-Rivoli or Pont Neuf

IN **THE KNOW**

The ringing of **St.-Germain l'Auxerrois's bells** signaled the start of the St. Bartholomew's Day Massacre (August 23, 1572) during the Wars of Religion. More than 3,000 Protestant Huguenots were killed in Paris—and more than 70,000 across France—at the behest of the Catholic Queen Catherine de Médicis and her son King Charles IX.

Rue de Rivoli

2 The covered arches of Paris's main street stretch for 1 mile (1.6 km), from Place de la Concorde (see p. 134) to Place du Louvre, and cover a rich mixture of cafés, restaurants, elegant shopping, and souvenir shops. Napoleon I commissioned this wide street in 1811 to commemorate his victory over the Austrian army at Rivoli, Italy, in 1797. The arcades have a pleasing classical uniformity and include stores such as **WHSmith** *(No. 248)* —Paris's largest English-language bookshop—and **Galignani**

(No. 224)—the first English bookshop on the continent (founded in 1802, although it settled in its current location in 1856). **Chez Angelina** *(No. 226)* is a perennially popular tearoom famous for its thick hot chocolate. For high-end shopping, try **Dolce & Gabbana** *(No. 244)* or **Sephora** *(No. 99)*, a Parisian cosmetics store. A gilded equestrian statue of the French heroine, **Joan of Arc,** stands at Place des Pyramides, close to where she was wounded in 1429 while fighting the English. Today, the statue is still a place of pilgrimage for French royalists.

From Place de la Concorde to rue St.-Antoine, 1st arr. • Métro: Louvre-Rivoli or Hôtel de Ville

The rue de Rivoli's elegant arcades shelter a selection of designer stores and cafés.

Musée des Arts Décoratifs

3 In the northwestern wing of the Louvre is a museum focusing on decorative French objects. Around 150,000 items from religious and everyday life are on display, including toys, stained glass, furniture, ceramics, and jewelry, all dating from the medieval period to the 20th century. The extensive **doll collection** on the fifth floor is exceptional. Another highlight is the **Galerie des Bijoux**—two rooms, connected by a breathtaking glass bridge, which hold a historic collection of 1,200 rings, necklaces, bracelets, and brooches. The entrance fee includes admission to the adjoining **Musée de la Mode et du Textile,** which has rotating collections exploring the French fashion industry from the 17th to the 20th centuries—including world-famous Parisian haute couture (see pp. 140–141), and to the **Musée de la Publicité,** which tells the history of advertising and has an extensive collection of posters. The café has wonderful views across the Jardin des Tuileries.

107 rue de Rivoli, 1st arr. • www.lesartsdecoratifs.fr • 01 44 55 57 50 • €€
• Closed Mon. • Métro: Palais-Royal Musée du Louvre

Musée du Louvre

4 See pp. 122–125.

Rue de Rivoli, 1st arr. • www.louvre.fr • 01 40 20 53 17 • €€ • Closed Tues., Jan. 1, May 1, and Dec. 25 • Métro: Palais-Royal Musée du Louvre

Jardin des Tuileries

5 The formal lawns and woodland spaces of this 63-acre (25 ha) garden on the banks of the Seine are all that remain of the Palais des Tuileries, which linked the two wings of the Louvre. Queen Catherine de Médicis started the garden in the 16th century. Landscape designer André Le Nôtre, who laid out the park at Versailles for Louis XIV, redesigned the garden in the 17th century, creating the central axis that runs from the Louvre west toward the Champs-Élysées. In 1667 the garden opened to the public. Today,

You have to be quick to get a chair at the Jardin des Tuileries, especially in summer.

THE LOUVRE & PALAIS-ROYAL

with its fountains and ponds, formal flowerbeds, benches and cafés, and numerous statues, including **20 bronzes** by 20th-century French artist Aristide Maillol, it remains a popular oasis. Atop the **Arc de Triomphe du Carrousel,** at the garden's eastern end, is a striking statue of Napoleon I in a chariot drawn by four horses. Napoleon commissioned the arch in 1806 as an entrance to the Palais des Tuileries and to commemorate his victories. During the 1871 uprisings, revolutionaries torched the Tuileries (the Louvre survived), opening up a superb view known as the **Triumphal Way.** From the Arc de Triomphe du Carrousel you can look west through the gardens to the Luxor Obelisk—a gift from the Egyptian government in the 19th century—in the Place de la Concorde. Or look up the Champs-Élysées to the Arc de Triomphe (see pp. 138–139) and beyond to the Grande Arche de La Défense, 5 miles (8 km) away.

Rue de Rivoli, 1st arr. • Métro: Tuileries

Musée de l'Orangerie

6 Citrus trees originally grew in the orangerie in the southwest corner of the Jardin des Tuileries, yet it is now more famous for housing Claude Monet's **"Nymphéas,"** a series of eight water-lily paintings. Painted between 1914 and 1918, toward the end of Monet's life, they offer a stunning evocation of the beauty of his garden at Giverny, 43 miles (69 km) west of Paris. The vast scale of the water-lily paintings, exhibited on the top floor, are impressive. Each painting is 6 feet (1.8 m) high, and they are arranged in two groups, one representing dusk, the other, sunrise. They were first put on display when the museum opened in 1927, shortly after the artist's death, and are acknowledged to be among the greatest works of 20th-century art. Following a renovation of the museum in 2006, natural light now washes over these masterworks, with weather playing with the paintings in the way the artist intended. The museum also houses modern art collected by Parisian dealer Paul Guillaume, including pieces by Pablo Picasso, Francis Picabia,

Chaïm Soutine, Marie Laurencin, and Pierre-Auguste Renoir. Highlights include Paul Cézanne's **"Apples and Cookies"** (Room 3) and Henri Rousseau's **"Old Junier's Cart"** (Room 4). The museum also hosts changing exhibitions of 20th-century art.

Jardin des Tuileries, 8th arr. • www.musee-orangerie.fr • 01 44 77 80 07 • €€ • Closed Tues., May 1, and Dec. 25 • Guided tours are held in English Mon. and Thurs. at 2:30 p.m. (€€) • Métro: Concorde

Galerie Nationale du Jeu de Paume

7 Across the Jardin des Tuileries from the Musée de l'Orangerie, this former indoor tennis court is now used by the Centre National de la Photographie, with exhibits on photography and cinema. Constructed in 1851 by Napoleon III as a copy of the Orangerie, the Jeu de Paume (literally, "game of the palm"—from the time when players hit the ball with the palm of the hand) became a gallery in 1919. In 1986, much of its collection moved to the Musée d'Orsay (see pp. 154–155) and the new Musée d'Art Moderne (Museum of Modern Art; *11 ave. du Président Wilson, 16th arr., www.mam.paris.fr, 01 53 67 40 00, closed Mon. and public holidays*). After a period of rebuilding, the new Jeu de Paume opened its doors in 2002 with a series of highly popular exhibitions by major figures in the world of photography such as Richard Avedon, Martin Parr, Lee Miller, and André Kertész. The museum shows work by emerging artists and has an international program of collaborative curatorial work. It also has a sister site for temporary exhibitions at the **Hôtel de Béthune-Sully** (see p. 100).

Jardin des Tuileries, 8th arr. • www.jeudepaume.org • 01 47 03 12 50 • Closed Mon., Jan. 1, May 1, and Dec. 25 • €€ • Métro: Concorde

GOOD **EATS**

■ **L'ÉPI D'OR**
A traditional bistro a short walk from the Louvre, this is a rare survivor from the days when the Les Halles food market was open. Good value. **25 rue Jean-Jacques Rousseau, 1st arr., 01 42 36 38 12, €**

■ **LE FUMOIR**
Chic Parisians come to this large and comfortable restaurant-bar, situated within seconds of the Louvre, for brunch, dinner, or a late-night martini. **6 rue de l'Amiral de Coligny, 1st arr., 01 42 92 00 24, €€**

■ **LE RUBIS**
On a street of restaurants near the Jardin des Tuileries, this bistro remains a favorite with business people at lunch and a fashionable crowd in the evening. **10 rue Marché St.-Honoré, 1st arr., 01 42 61 03 34, €€**

THE LOUVRE & PALAIS-ROYAL

Palais-Royal (and Le Grand Véfour)

8 This 17th-century palace, originally built for Cardinal Richelieu, has had a tempestuous history. Under the ownership of Louis-Philippe-Joseph, Duke of Orléans, the Jardin du Palais-Royal (Royal Palace Garden) was at the center of Paris's social scene, with merchants, intellectuals, prostitutes, and people from all walks of life—except the police, whom the duke had banned—filling its arcade of shops, cafés, gambling dens, restaurants, and theaters. Today, although smaller than the original built for the cardinal in 1633, the garden retains a formal 17th-century design with lime-tree-lined avenues and a central fountain. While the antiques shops that once dominated the gardens are still there, many have given way to art galleries, perfumeries, shoe shops, and high-end fashion retailers such as Stella McCartney and Marc Jacobs. The adjacent courtyard boasts a controversial installation of black-and-white striped columns, called **"Les Deux Plateaux,"** by French artist Daniel Buren. The **Comédie Française** (*Place Colette, 1st arr., www.comedie-francaise.fr, 08 25 10 16 80*), a state-run theater, has been in the Palais-Royal since 1799. The main palace buildings house government offices and are closed to visitors. The sole survivor of the pre-revolutionary restaurants is **Le Grand Véfour** (*rue de Beaujolais, 01 42 96 56 27, closed Aug., €€€€€*) on the garden's north side, founded in 1784 as the Café de Chartres. Brass plaques on the walls mark the preferred tables of French national heroes Napoleon Bonaparte, Victor Hugo (who ate the same dish for more than 30 years—steak and potatoes with green beans), and Jean-Paul Sartre, among others. The restaurant, run by chef Guy Martin, is now Michelin-starred.

Garden entrances: rue de Montpensier, rue de Beaujolais/ Passage Perron, rue de Valois, 8th arr. • Métro: Pyramides

Daniel Buren's "Les Deux Plateaux" has become a popular place to relax and have fun.

Musée du Louvre

*Paris's grandest palace holds one of the world's
most significant collections of historic art.*

"Artemis with a Doe" was first displayed at the Louvre when the building was a royal palace.

The Louvre is not only one of the world's great museums, it is one of the
world's great historical sites. The palace was home to medieval kings and,
in the mid-19th century, to Emperor Napoleon III. Although the monarchs
are gone, it has retained the impressive art collections of its former residents.
Today, thousands of beautiful and historically significant works of art are on
display. Despite its size, many visitors flock to its most famous exhibits,
which are often surrounded by a melee of tourists.

■ GREEK ANTIQUITIES

In Room 12 of the ground floor of the Sully Wing, you'll find the smooth and sumptuously draped curves of the **"Venus de Milo."** Despite the loss of her arms during her almost 2,000-year existence, she is one of the world's most famous antique sculptures.

Next door to the Venus is another monument of ancient Greek art: a section of the Athenian **Parthenon Frieze** (Room 6, Ground Floor, Sully Wing). This extraordinarily well-preserved relief depicts young women participating in a ceremony to honor Athena, goddess of wisdom. The finely carved figures wear robes that are so delicate it is difficult to believe they are made of marble. Best of all, most people rush by the Parthenon fragments on their way to see the Venus de Milo, giving the visitor ample time and space to enjoy a treasure of ancient art.

■ EGYPTIAN & ANCIENT NEAR EASTERN ANTIQUITIES

As with every encyclopedic museum, the mummy- and sphinx-filled galleries are always crowded. A particular highlight of the Louvre's Egyptian collection is **"The God Amun Protecting Tutankhamun"** (Room 26, First Floor, Pharaonic

Egypt), which experts think is a faithful portrait of the young pharaoh.

The museum's collection of ancient Near Eastern Antiquities is perhaps even stronger than its Egyptian holdings. And the artwork here is displayed in galleries that are not filled to capacity with tourists. Room 4 in the Mesopotamian galleries—also called the Cour Khorsabad—is particularly striking. This room features wall reliefs and guard figures from an eighth-century B.C. wall that surrounded the city of Dur Sharrukin (present-day Khorsabad, northern Iraq). Among these ancient carvings are two enormous **Winged Human-Headed Bulls.** These creatures are 13 feet (4 m) tall and 13 feet (4 m) wide, and would have stood at one of the seven gates to the city. They offered supernatural protection and served an architectural purpose as key structural supports for the gateway and wall.

THE LOUVRE & PALAIS-ROYAL

■ Renaissance Art

The long **Grand Gallery** is the Louvre's main byway, at the center of a network of rooms that contain many of the collection's painted masterpieces. If you approach the Grand Gallery from the staircase housing the ancient Greek statue of Nike, the **"Winged Victory of Samothrace"** (Escalier Daru, Ground Floor, Denon Wing), you will come to Fra Angelico's **"The Coronation of the Virgin"** (Room 3, First Floor, Denon Wing). This glowing, multicolored 15th-century altarpiece was painted for a Dominican monastery near Florence.

Both the diverse crowd of onlookers and the elaborate marble and gilt design will entertain the visitor's eye.

Moving through the gallery, you will likely see a crowd in front of Raphael's charming **"La Jardinière"** (Room 8, First Floor, Denon Wing), a painting of the Virgin playing with the Christ child and his cousin John the Baptist. Having seen this Madonna, look along the opposite wall for his **"Portrait of Baldassare Castiglione,"** a friend of Raphael and ambassador to the pope from the Duke of Urbino. Castiglione's fur stole is meticulously

In Jacques-Louis David's "The Coronation of Napoleon," the emperor crowns his kneeling wife.

rendered, and his ice-blue eyes are piercing while maintaining a certain warmth. Leonardo da Vinci's **"La Gioconda,"** better known as **"Mona Lisa"** (Room 6, First Floor, Denon Wing), is undoubtedly the Louvre's most famous painting. You will be able to catch a glimpse of the famous smile amid the crowds—but you should also spend time with other magnificent works that do not attract such attention.

The "Mona Lisa" has an entire wall to herself and holds court behind bulletproof glass.

■ FRENCH PAINTINGS

Rooms 75 and 77, accessible through the doorway just behind the "Mona Lisa," are home to the great masterpieces of French neoclassical and romantic art. And while these rooms are crowded, the enormous paintings are large enough for everyone to see. The largest and arguably most dramatic among these is Théodore Géricault's **"The Raft of the Medusa"** (Room 77, First Floor, Denon Wing), which depicts the plight of the victims of a contemporary shipwreck. A group of survivors clings to the raft as it is battered by the waves, and one of them signals with a white cloth at a barely visible boat on the horizon.

To create this scene, Géricault mixed bitumen into his colors to create deep, dark shadows. Unfortunately, this black wrinkles with time and, despite frequent conservation, the painting gradually becomes darker and less legible.

Other paintings here include Jacques-Louis David's **"Oath of the Horatii"** (Room 75, First Floor, Denon Wing), depicting Roman warriors saluting their father as they preparing to fight, and Eugène Delacroix's **"Liberty Leading the People"** (Room 77, First Floor, Denon Wing), an eyewitness account of the 1830 revolution.

Rue de Rivoli, 1st arr. • www.louvre.fr • 01 40 20 53 17 • €€ • Closed Tues., Jan. 1, May 1, and Dec. 25 • Métro: Palais-Royal Musée du Louvre

Royal Architecture

Despite the execution of the king and his family during the French Revolution, Paris is indelibly stamped with royal buildings. Clovis I, first king of the Franks, established his capital here in A.D. 508, but it was the medieval monarchs who cemented the city's position as a royal stronghold, bestowing palaces and cathedrals on a city whose later inhabitants burned a few down and didn't always seem to appreciate them.

The Bassin d'Apollon fountain at Versailles (above) dates from 1671. The palace's golden fence (right) is a copy, installed in 2008. The original was torn down during the French Revolution.

Island Stronghold

After Frankish kings chose the Île de la Cité as their capital during the Middle Ages, the island became the primary seat of French royalty. All that remains today of the palace that dominated the island are **La Conciergerie** (see pp. 44–45) and the nearby **Ste.-Chapelle** (see p. 45), two of the oldest (and finest) examples of Gothic architecture in Europe.

Royal Expansion

When the throne passed to the House of Valois in 1328, the Île de la Cité's grip on royal affairs waned. King Charles V relocated the royal court to the **Louvre** (see pp. 122–125), a medieval castle that was gradually remade into a Renaissance palace. Charles also commissioned the Bastille (see pp. 100 and 108–109), which four centuries later would play a key role in the city's history, and a royal residence in the Marais, the Hôtel St.-Paul that no longer exists. Following his example, many of the Valois kings frequented the Marais.

THE LOUVRE & PALAIS-ROYAL

In the mid-16th century, Queen Catherine de Médicis moved the royal court back near the Seine, where she created the Palais des Tuileries and its garden (see pp. 118–119) adjacent to the Louvre.

A Move to the Country

In 1589, the monarchy passed from the Valois to the Bourbons. King Louis XIII continued expansion of the Louvre-Tuileries palace, but in 1624 he built a hunting lodge near a little-known village called **Versailles.** Not much happened with the property until his son assumed the throne in 1643. For a time, the young Louis XIV lived in the Palais-Royal, but he would soon transform Versailles into Europe's greatest palace (*Place d'Armes, Versailles, www .chateauversailles.fr, 01 30 83 78 00, €€€/€€€€€, closed Mon., Jan. 1, Easter Mon., May 1, June 13, Aug. 15, and Dec. 25*).

NAPOLEON'S **PARIS**

When Napoleon Bonaparte declared himself emperor in 1804, he made the Louvre-Tuileries palace his primary residence. His most conspicuous creation is the Arc de Triomphe (see pp. 138–139), yet he also remade the neighborhood north of the Louvre, creating rue de Rivoli (see pp. 116–117), the victory column in Place Vendôme (made from captured canon), and La Madeleine church (*Place de la Madeleine, 8th arr.*).

THE LOUVRE & PALAIS-ROYAL

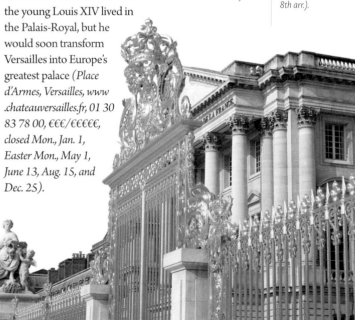

Prêt-à-Porter

Paris is one of the world's premier shopping cities, famous for its elegant style and chic fashion. The city that brought the world haute couture (see pp. 140–141) also does prêt-à-porter (ready-to-wear) fashion extremely well. For a sample of the best shops in Paris, try on some of these suggestions for size.

■ DEPARTMENT STORES

Paris has some of the world's oldest department stores, and also some of the most exclusive. Parisian fashionistas shop at **Colette** (*213 rue St.-Honoré, 1st arr., www.colette.fr, 01 55 35 33 90, closed Sun.*) for cutting-edge clothing. The city's oldest department store, **Le Bon Marché** (*24 rue de Sèvres, 7th arr., 01 44 39 80 00, closed Sun.*) opened in 1838 and features more than 40 designers, including Sandro, Maje, and Dice Kayek; comprehensive lingerie and beauty sections; and an excellent wedding boutique. The art deco building has retained its original splendor. Another favorite is **Galeries Lafayette** (*40 blvd. Haussmann, 9th arr., 01 42 82 34 56, closed Sun.*), which stocks labels such as agnès b, Derhy, and Hugo Boss. It also has good menswear and children's sections. The latest department store to arrive in Paris is a concept shop unlike anything else in the city: **Merci** (*111 blvd. Beaumarchais, 3rd arr., 01 42 77 00 33, closed Sun.*) has loft-style spaces amply stocked with clothes including designs by Stella McCartney and Isabel Marant. There is also an excellent café.

■ INDEPENDENT BOUTIQUES

Kamille (*1 place Alphonse Deville, 6th arr., www.kamilleparis.fr, 01 45 44 35 67, closed Sun.*) is a small shop filled with unique clothes, handpicked by the owner from a wide range of European designers. For whimsical, uplifting clothing, try **Antoine et Lili** (*95 quai de Valmy, 10th arr., www.antoineetlili .com, 01 40 37 41 55*), whose colorful shop contains bohemian designs with exotic influences. **L'Éclaireur** (*40 rue de Sévigné, 3rd arr., www.leclaireur.com, 01 48 87 10 22, closed Sun.*) is worth a trip just for the futuristic interior, although the edgy fashion may not appeal to everyone. **Paul & Joe** (*62–66*

Antoine et Lili's fuschia-pink interior displays equally colorful clothes.

rue des Sts.-Pères, 6th arr., www.paul andjoe.com, 01 42 22 47 01, closed Sun.) offers eclectic and very French designs for women, men, and children—plus a makeup line. The trendy menswear section is excellent. **Comptoir des Cotonniers** *(2 place St.-Sulpice, 6th arr., www.comptoirdes cotonniers.com, 01 56 81 00 18, closed Sun.)* has boutiques all over Paris, offering clothes that are affordable and casually chic. Understated and hip, **Isabel Marant** *(16 rue de Charonne, 11th arr., www.isabelmarant.tm.fr, 01 49 29 71 55)* has been producing fabulous fashion since the young age

of 15. For simple yet classic Parisian style, head to **Autour du Monde** *(8 rue des Francs Bourgeois, 3rd arr., www .autourdumonde.com, 01 42 77 06 08, closed Sun.),* whose Bensimon collection has a line of effortless yet sassy clothing, canvas shoes, perfumes, and related accessories.

■ SHOES & HANDBAGS
Pring's *(9 rue Charlot, 3rd arr., www.pringparis.com, 01 42 72 71 87, closed Sun.)* unmistakable shoes and handbags are handcrafted in the designer's studio from materials such as snakeskin, lambskin, and kidskin.

Champs-Élysées

Running through one of Paris's most prestigious areas in the west of the city center, France's most famous boulevard literally translates as "avenue of the Elysian Fields." The original eastern section was designed by Queen Marie de Médicis in 1616, and it is still bounded by celestially inspired gardens. Since extended, this 1.2-mile-long (2 km) tree-lined promenade, which hosts the Bastille Day procession, boasts some of the city's most elegant cafés, shops, and restaurants—making it a favorite place for both Parisians and tourists to go for an evening stroll. The eastern end is anchored by Place de la Concorde, Paris's largest square and site of many revolutionary executions. At the other end stands the colossal Arc de Triomphe—now the site of France's Tomb of the Unknown Soldier from World War I. The ornate Petit Palais and Grand Palais, both built for the 1900 Universal Exhibition, are still used for art shows and events. More fabulous art can be found at Musée Jacquemart-André—a fine example of the area's many ornate 19th-century mansions.

❰ **One of two monumental, 19th-century fountains gracing the Place de la Concorde**

Champs-Élysées

One of the world's most beautiful boulevards has some of Paris's most recognizable sights, as well as street cafés, shops, and fine restaurants.

❺ Cathédrale St. Alexandre-Nevsky (see pp. 135–136) This Russian Orthodox cathedral has an interior decorated with icons, mosaics, and frescoes. Continue on rue Daru, turn left onto rue de Courcelles and then right onto boulevard de Courcelles.

❹ Arc de Triomphe (see pp. 138–139) Commissioned by Napoleon I, this monumental arch at the northwest end of the Champs-Élysées honors those who fought for France in the Revolutionary and Napoleonic Wars. Walk east up avenue Hoche, turn left onto rue du Faubourg St.-Honoré and then right onto rue Daru.

Monceau

BOULEVARD DE COURCELLES

PLACE DES TERNES

Ⓜ Ternes

Ⓜ Courcelles

Parc Monceau

❻

RUE DE COURCELLES

AVENUE DE WAGRAM

❺ Cathédrale St.-Alexandre-Nevsky

AVENUE HOCHE

Arc de Triomphe

❹

PLACE CHARLES DE GAULLE

Ⓜ Charles de Gaulle Étoile

AVENUE DE FRIEDLAND

RUE L

AVENUE DES CHAMPS-ÉLYSÉES

Ⓜ George V

AVENUE GEORGE V

RUE FRANÇOIS 1ER

Franklin D. Roosevelt

AVENUE MONTAIGNE

RUE FRANÇOIS

Ⓜ Alma Marceau

PLACE DE L'ALMA

COURS ALBERT 1ER

PORT DE LA CONFÉRENC

Seine

**CHAMPS-ÉLYSÉES   DISTANCE: 2.9 MILES (4.7 KM)
TIME: APPROX. 8 HOURS MÉTRO START: CONCORDE**

6 Parc Monceau (see p. 136) This English-style garden is full of pyramids, pagodas, and other follies of 18th-century landscape design. Leave the park via rue Rembrandt on the south side, turn south onto rue de Courcelles, then east onto boulevard Haussmann.

7 Musée Jacquemart-André (see pp. 136–137) State apartments, private chambers, and a winter garden house exquisite paintings, tapestries, and sculptures of predominantly French, Italian, and Dutch art from the 16th to 18th centuries.

Musée
Jacquemart-André

BOULEVARD HAUSSMANN

Miromesnil Ⓜ

St.-Augustin Ⓜ

FAUBOURG ST.-HONORÉ

Ⓜ St.-Philippe
du Roule

BOULEVARD MALESHERBES

AVENUE MATIGNON

AVENUE DE MARIGNY

ROND POINT
DES CHAMPS-ÉLYSÉES
MARCEL DASSAULT

Champs-Élysées
Clémenceau Ⓜ

AVE. DES CHAMPS - ÉLYSÉES

Grand
Palais

③

AVE. FRANKLIN
D. ROOSEVELT

AVE. WINSTON CHURCHILL

Petit
Palais

②

Concorde Ⓜ

①

Place de la
Concorde

PONT ALEXANDRE III

PONT DES
CHAMPS-ÉLYSÉES

PORT DES
CHAMPS-ÉLYSÉES

PONT DE LA
CONCORDE

PONT
DES INVALIDES

0   500 meters
0   500 yards

1 Place de la Concorde (see p. 134) Start at Paris's largest square, where the guillotine worked overtime during the French Revolution. Walk up the avenue des Champs-Élysées, and turn south onto avenue Winston Churchill.

2 Petit Palais (see p. 134) On your left is the smaller of the two palaces built for the Universal Exhibition of 1900. The Musée des Beaux-Arts de la Ville de Paris shows art from antiquity to the 20th century. Cross over avenue Winston Churchill.

3 Grand Palais (see p. 135) The Grand Palais combines three exhibition spaces: Galeries Nationales (temporary art shows), Palais de la Découverte (science museum), and La Nef (grand events). Return to the Champs-Élysées and head west.

CHAMPS-ÉLYSÉES

The 75-foot-tall (23 m) Luxor Obelisk was a gift from Egypt in 1826.

Place de la Concorde

1 Paris's largest square is bordered by the Jardin des Tuileries (see pp. 118–119), the Seine, and the 18th-century facade of the Hôtel de Crillon (see p. 184). The 20-acre (8 ha) space was created in 1754 to display a statue of King Louis XV. During the French Revolution a guillotine replaced the statue—more than 2,800 people were killed here, including King Louis XVI and his wife Marie-Antoinette. When the square was redesigned in the 1830s, the **Luxor Obelisk,** an ancient obelisk from Ramses II's temple at Luxor, was installed along with two fountains. The **Fountain of the Rivers,** on the north side, represents the Rhône and the Rhine, and the **Maritime Fountain** pays homage to France's seafaring spirit.

Southeast end of ave. des Champs-Élysées, 8th arr.
• Métro: Concorde

Petit Palais

2 With a blend of neoclassical and beaux-arts architecture, the "Little Palace" is a work of art to rival the masterpieces held within. The garden portico has frescoes depicting the months of the year and the hours of the day, while French 20th-century artist Maurice Denis painted the portraits of famous artists in the cupola. Visit one of the temporary exhibitions or take your pick of the permanent collection: Greek and Roman antiquities, religious work from the Middle Ages, Renaissance art, 17th-century Dutch paintings, and French work spanning the 18th to 20th centuries. Highlights include Paul Cézanne's **"Four Seasons"** (Room 8) and Claude Monet's **"Sunset on the Seine in Winter"** (Room 7).

1 ave. Winston Churchill, 8th arr. • www.petitpalais.paris.fr • 01 53 43 40 00
• Temporary exhibitions: some free, some €€ • Closed Mon. and public holidays
• Métro: Champs-Élysées Clémenceau

Grand Palais

3 This masterpiece of engineering has it all: beaux-arts architecture, a neoclassical stone facade, ornate art-nouveau ironwork, and a series of allegorical statues. The interior is bathed in light from Europe's largest glass ceiling. The structure was built (along with the Petit Palais) to hold the Universal Exhibition of 1900, with 40 artists creating sculptures, friezes, and other embellishments, such as the **monumental bronze chariots** that take pride of place above each wing of the main facade. **La Nef** (The Nave), at the heart of the complex, hosts major events and art shows staged on a grand scale. The building also includes the **Galeries Nationales** (*ave. Winston Churchill, 01 44 13 17 17, €€*), which holds temporary exhibitions, and the **Palais de la Découverte** (*ave. Franklin D. Roosevelt, 01 56 43 20 20, €€*), a museum and planetarium with displays on math, physics, electromagnetism, and other sciences.

Ave. Winston Churchill, 8th arr. • www.grandpalais.fr • Closed Tues., May 1, and Dec. 25 • Métro: Champs-Élysées Clémenceau

Arc de Triomphe

4 See pp. 138–139.

Place Charles de Gaulle, 8th arr. • www.arcdetriompheparis.com • 01 55 37 73 77 • €€ • Closed May 8, July 14, and Nov. 11 (a.m.); Jan. 1, May 1, and Dec. 25 (all day) • Métro: Charles de Gaulle Étoile

Cathédrale St. Alexandre-Nevsky

5 This striking Russian-Orthodox cathedral was inspired by the church architecture of Novgorod and Moscow. Consecrated in 1861, it was funded by Paris's Russian expatriate community, which had grown rapidly following the defeat of Napoleon I, as well as by a personal donation from Tsar Alexander II. The building takes the form of a cross and is topped with five golden domes representing Christ and the four Evangelists. The interior is richly ornamented with icons, mosaics, and frescoes, including the ornate fresco in the central cupola, which depicts Christ, the Virgin, and numerous saints—the other domes show scenes from the life of Christ. Services are still conducted in Russian.

12 rue Daru, 8th arr. • 01 42 27 37 34 • Open Tues. and Fri. 1 p.m.–5 p.m.; services Sat. 6 p.m., Sun. 10 a.m. • Métro: Ternes or Courcelles

GOOD **EATS**

■ LADURÉE
Elegant tearoom founded in 1862, famous for its pastries and chocolates. It also serves lunch. **75 ave. des Champs-Élysées, 8th arr., 01 40 75 08 75, €€**

■ SPOON
Fusion bistro just off the Champs-Élysées run by three-Michelin-star chef Alain Ducasse, with healthy, seasonal dishes. **12 rue de Marignan, 8th arr., 01 40 76 34 44, €€€€**

■ STELLA MARIS
Near the Arc de Triomphe, Stella Maris stands out for its classic French cuisine with subtle Asian notes. **4 rue Arsène Houssaye, 8th arr., 01 42 89 16 22, €€€€**

Parc Monceau

6 Designed in an English style, complete with follies and other architectural features, this unusual park does not conform to the formal style of most historic French gardens. It was created by Philippe d'Orléans, Duke of Chartres, in 1769 and was transformed into a public park by architect Georges-Eugène Haussmann in 1861. Today, a number of follies remain, including an Egyptian pyramid, a Chinese pagoda, and a Corinthian colonnade alongside an ornamental lake. After strolling in the park, head to the eastern edge to visit the **Musée Cernuschi** (*7 ave. Vélasquez, 8th arr., 01 53 96 21 50, temporary exhibitions: €€, closed Mon. and public holidays*). This collection of Asian art, originally assembled by 19th-century banker Henri Cernuschi, includes bronzes, ceramics, masks, and other pieces from China, Japan, and Korea—such as a fifth-century **Bodhisattva statue** and a **14th-century Buddha bell.** The museum also hosts temporary exhibitions of Asian art.

Blvd. de Courcelles, 8th arr. • Métro: Monceau

Musée Jacquemart-André

7 This 19th-century mansion was built by Édouard André and his wife Nélie Jacquemart to house their vast art collection. The state rooms contain 18th-century French art, including

CHAMPS-ÉLYSÉES

Louis XIV to Louis XVI furniture graces the Musée Jacquemart-André's Tapestry Room.

"**Allegory of Science**" by Jean-Baptiste-Siméon Chardin. Furniture from the Louis XIV to Louis XVI periods fill the informal rooms, as well as more fine art including the "**Russian Games**" tapestries by 18th-century French artist Jean-Baptiste Le Prince, "**The New Model**," (circa 1760) by painter Jean-Honoré Fragonard, and "**Christ at Emmaus**" (circa 1628) by the Dutch master Rembrandt. A fresco by Venetian artist Giambattista Tiepolo decorates the winter garden's staircase. The dining room (now the café) also has a Tiepolo ceiling. On the upper floor, the Italian Museum features work from the Italian Renaissance including "**Virgin and Child**" (circa 1465) by Sandro Botticelli, a painting of the same title by Giovanni Bellini, as well as sculptures by Donatello and Francesco Laurana. Temporary exhibitions are also held in the mansion.

158 blvd. Haussmann, 8th arr. • www.musee-jacquemart-andre.com • 01 45 62 11 59 • €€ • Métro: Miromesnil or St.-Philippe du Roule

Arc de Triomphe

*Scenes from Napoleon's victories decorate Paris's triumphant arch,
which stands above the Tomb of the Unknown Soldier.*

Traffic races around the Arc de Triomphe day and night.

Paris's most famous landmark after the Eiffel Tower honors those who fought
for France during the French Revolutionary and Napoleonic Wars. Plans for
the triumphal arch began in 1806, following Napoleon I's decisive victory over
the Russo-Austrian army at Austerlitz. The ambitious project was headed by
architect Jean-François-Thérèse Chalgrin; it took two years just to lay the
foundations, and the 162-foot-tall (49 m) arch wasn't completed until 1836.
It is the focal point for France's annual Bastille Day celebrations.

■ SCULPTURES

France's greatest sculptors of the early 19th century—Jean-Pierre Cortot, François Rude, Antoine Étex, and James Pradier—were commissioned to create works for the arch. The two sculptures on the west facade are "**The Resistance of 1814**" (on the right), and "**The Peace of 1815**" (both by Étex), while on the east facade are "**The Triumph of 1810**" (by Cortot, on the left) and the most renowned, "**Departure of the Volunteers of 1792**," commonly called La Marseillaise (by Rude).

■ THE RELIEFS

The six reliefs on the upper facades represent significant moments of the Revolutionary and Napoleonic Wars: battles at Aboukir, Jemappes, Arcole, and Austerlitz, the fall of Alexandria, and the burial of General Marceau.

■ TOP SECTION

The arcades are decorated with allegorical figures from Roman mythology (by Pradier). Above the frieze of soldiers are 30 shields engraved with the names of major Revolutionary and Napoleonic battles.

The inner facades of the smaller supporting arches list the names of 558 French generals; those who died in battle are underlined.

■ TOMB OF THE UNKNOWN SOLDIER

The body of an unidentified French casualty of World War I was laid to rest beneath the arch in 1921. The slab above carries the inscription: "Here lies a French soldier who died for his fatherland 1914–1918." The eternal flame is rekindled every evening at 6:30 p.m. and burns in memory of the dead from both World Wars who were never identified.

■ MUSEUM

An elevator takes visitors up to the attic, where there is a museum on the history of the arch. Another 46 steps bring you to a viewing platform on top of the arch, from which you can enjoy a panoramic view of Paris.

Place Charles de Gaulle, 8th arr. • www.arcdetriompheparis.com • 01 55 37 73 77 • €€ • Closed May 8, July 14, and Nov. 11 (a.m.); Jan. 1, May 1, and Dec. 25 (all day) • Métro: Charles de Gaulle Étoile

CHAMPS-ÉLYSÉES

Haute Couture

Paris has been synonymous with fine clothes for centuries. Haute couture (literally, "high dressmaking") is centered around the Champs-Élysées, and it is the most exclusive part of French fashion. Its roots are in the exuberant years of the Third Empire under Napoleon III and his wife Empress Eugénie, yet it was an Englishman, Charles Frederick Worth, who forged the present system when he founded his own label in 1854, selling dresses to fashionable ladies.

Chanel (above) has retained its trademark simple look; Jean Paul Gaultier's colorful shows combine high fashion and theater (opposite).

Little Black Dress

Gabrielle "Coco" Chanel opened her first store in 1913, with a revolutionary new style influenced by comfort and simplicity—a sharp break from the corseted clothing that had defined the 19th century. She is best known for the most iconic item ever to grace the catwalk—the Little Black Dress. The color had previously been reserved for funerals, but in 1926, Chanel shocked the fashion world with an elegant, sleeveless design that was cut just below the knee; it was an instant and everlasting success.

The New Look

Following World War II's hardships, fashion during the recovery of the 1950s was defined by Christian Dior's "New Look." Voluminous use of fabric, long skirts, and small shoulders and waists were used to create the classic "hour glass" shape. Dior's elegant, feminine designs captured the world's imagination, and although his dresses were impractical for most women, their influence kept Paris at the forefront of world fashion.

Haute Couture Fashion Shows

Today, haute-couture fashion shows still define the style for the following season. Every spring and autumn, the world's press, celebrities, and buyers gather to watch the shows. Not many can afford these clothes, however, as an original can cost hundreds of thousands of dollars.

Putting on a show is often a financial loss-making affair for the fashion houses, yet the publicity gained makes the vast expense of hiring teams of cutters, machinists, embroiderers, and seamstresses—not to mention the cost of the fabrics—worth it. Although the designs are not destined for the mass market, they can set trends which propel a fashion house's prêt-à-porter (ready-to-wear; see pp. 128–129) designs to global acclaim.

FASHION **HOUSES**

Adeline André Founded her fashion house in 1981.

Jean Paul Gaultier Founded in 1976. Jean Paul Gaultier is still the creative force.

Givenchy Founded by Hubert de Givenchy in 1952. Riccardo Ticci is now head of couture.

Stéphane Rolland One of the newest names to join haute couture, with a strong Middle-Eastern influence.

Yves Saint-Laurent An assistant to Dior, Saint-Laurent founded his own label in 1961 and became one of fashion's biggest names. The current head designer is Stefano Pilati.

City by Night

Paris became known as La Ville Lumière ("the city of light") during the Enlightenment, when it gained a reputation as a center of learning. Early adoption of street lighting—the Champs-Élysées was the first street in Europe to be gaslit—helped cement its nickname. Today, the city is at its most magical after sunset.

■ PLACE DE LA CONCORDE

At night, **Cleopatra's Needle** glows pink as the square is gently illuminated by hundreds of old-fashioned street-lamps. As you gaze west down the **Champs-Élysées,** the distant **Arc de Triomphe** (see pp. 138–139) stands out like a beacon against the darkness. To the east, the **Place du Carrousel,** with its own triumphal arch, and to the north, the twin buildings of the **Meurice** and **Crillon** hotels, are all wonderfully lit up. Also aglow is the neoclassical portico of the **Assemblée Nationale** (*126 rue de l'Université, 7th arr.*), home to the lower house of French government, to the south.

■ ÎLE DE LA CITÉ

The pont de la Tournelle on the south side of the Île St.-Louis provides a good view of the city and **Cathédrale de Notre-Dame de Paris** (see pp. 48–49). Floodlights have been placed around the spires, arches, statues, and gargoyles of this masterpiece of gothic architecture, creating a sense of drama in the darkness.

La Conciergerie (see pp. 44–45), the brooding 14th-century castle where Queen Marie-Antoinette spent her last night before execution, is bathed in beams of light that playfully reflect in the river. Its conical twin towers and imposing stone masonry are vividly lit, making the former prison seem even more dramatic.

■ MUSÉE DU LOUVRE

Both of the Louvre's courtyards (see pp. 122–125) are lit at night, with subtle shadows highlighting the elegance of the building's Renaissance facades. The subdued lighting in the romantic **Cour Carrée** bathes the buildings in soft, warm hues. In the larger **Cour Napoléon,** the I. M. Pei-designed glass pyramid has a magical charm, its translucent form playing with the lights.

Floodlights pick out the detailed gilding on one of the fountains in Place de la Concorde.

■ Tour Eiffel

Since 2000, the tower (see p. 149) has incorporated two illumination systems: the static lighting from 336 600W sodium lamp projectors and the sparkle lighting that runs for five minutes every hour on the hour beginning at 8 p.m. The Champ de Mars provides a good view, but the best one is from the terrace of the Palais de Chaillot (*Place du Trocadéro*), on the other side of the Seine. From here you have one of the best views in Paris— looking across the river to the Tour Eiffel and the **École Militaire** (see p. 150) beyond.

■ Les Invalides

The golden dome of Les Invalides' **Église du Dôme** (see pp. 151–152) is visible from all along the Seine, but to enjoy its full glory when floodlit, view it from Place Vauban on the south side.

■ Sacré-Coeur

Being constructed of travertine, which remains a weather-resistant white, Montmartre's great basilica (see pp. 168–169) appears to float as on a cloud above the city. If you visit Montmartre at night, take the steps or funicular up to Sacré-Coeur for a panoramic view of the floodlit city.

Tour Eiffel & Les Invalides

Grand landmarks dominate the 7th arrondissement, from the Tour Eiffel and the brilliant gold-topped Invalides to the sprawling 18th-century École Militaire. Occupying a prime position on the banks of the Seine River, the Musée d'Orsay is housed in a former railway station built in 1900. The newest addition to the area, Musée du Quai Branly, boasts a contemporary design that smoothly blends into the surrounding garden. Its rooftop restaurant affords an unparalleled view of the nearby Tour Eiffel. Since the 17th century, the French upper class gravitated toward the 7th district—the château that now houses the Musée Rodin dates from the early 1700s—and the area is still wealthy today, with quiet apartment buildings, discreet upmarket restaurants, and restrained nightlife.

◀ **Bestriding the Paris skyline, the Tour Eiffel symbolizes the romance of Paris.**

TOUR EIFFEL & LES INVALIDES

Tour Eiffel & Les Invalides

The Tour Eiffel and gold-topped Les Invalides anchor this aristocratic community.

❷ Musée du Quai Branly (see pp. 48–149) Devoted to non-European art, Paris's newest museum opened in 2006. Continue on Quai Branly.

❸ Tour Eiffel (see p. 149) Gustave Eiffel's tower created controversy upon its opening in 1889. Stroll southeast through the Champ de Mars.

❹ Parc du Champ de Mars (see p. 150) A former parade ground is now an attractive garden. Leave at the southeastern end and cross avenue de la Motte Picquet.

❺ École Militaire (see p. 150) The Military Academy was founded by King Louis XV in 1751. Cross Place de Fontenoy.

❻ UNESCO (see pp. 150–151) Modern sculptures are scattered through the UNESCO headquarters' gardens. Walk northeast on avenue de Lowendal.

❼ Les Invalides & Musée de l'Armée (see pp. 151–152) Napoleon's tomb lies beneath the gold-domed chapel. Cross boulevard des Invalides.

**TOUR EIFFEL & LES INVALIDES DISTANCE: 4 MILES (6.5 KM)
TIME: APPROX. 8 HOURS MÉTRO START: MUSÉE D'ORSAY**

TOUR EIFFEL & LES INVALIDES

1 **Musée d'Orsay** (see pp. 154–155)
The museum specializes in 19th-century art and design. It is rich in Impressionist paintings. Walk west on Quai Anatole France and Quai d'Orsay to Quai Branly.

8 **Musée Rodin**
(see pp. 152–153) This château museum houses dozens of sculptures by Auguste Rodin.

Map labels:

PONT DES INVALIDES
PONT ALEXANDRE III
QUAI D'ORSAY
PLACE DE FINLANDE
Invalides Ⓜ
Seine
QUAI ANATOLE FRANCE
Assemblée Nationale Ⓜ
ESPLANADE DES INVALIDES
AVE. DU MARÉCHAL GALLIENI
Musée d'Orsay
BOULEVARD ST-GERMAIN
Latour Maubourg Ⓜ
PLACE DES INVALIDES
Solférino Ⓜ
Les Invalides and Musée de l'Armée **7**
Varenne Ⓜ
BOULEVARD DES INVALIDES
JARDIN DE L'INTENDANT
Musée Rodin **8**
Rue du Bac Ⓜ
AVENUE DE TOURVILLE
PLACE VAUBAN
AVE DE VILLARS
St-François Xavier Ⓜ
BOULEVARD RASPAIL
Sèvres-Babylone Ⓜ
AVENUE DE SÉGUR
AVE. DE BRETEUIL
LOWENDAL
PLACE ANDRE TARDIEU
JARDIN CATHERINE LABOURÉ
SQUARE BOUCICAUT
AVENUE DUQUESNE
AVENUE DE BRETEUIL
BLVD DES INVALIDES
RUE DE SÈVRES
AVENUE DE SAXE
PLACE DE BRETEUIL
Duroc Ⓜ
RUE DE SÈVRES
PLACE HENRI QUEUILLE

0   500 meters
0   500 yards

Musée d'Orsay

1 See pp. 154–155.

1 rue de la Légion d'Honneur, 7th arr. • www.musee-orsay.fr • 01 40 49 48 14
• €€, special exhibitions: €€ • Closed Mon. • Métro: Solférino

Musée du Quai Branly

2 In a city chock-full of age-old structures and museums, it is unusual to discover a 21st-century museum that blends with its surroundings. At the Musée du Quai Branly, architect Jean Nouvel has achieved this feat through the use of tall glass panels and tiers of multicolored boxes on the exterior and one wall that has been embedded with lush foliage to create a **vertical garden**. The Branly features indigenous art from Asia, Oceania, Africa, and the Americas, including headdresses, masks, statues, totems, costumes, textiles, and musical instruments. As you wander through the exhibits, which are arranged by region, watch for headdresses from Alaska, sculptures

Masks from Southeast Asia in the Musée du Quai Branly

from Mexico, feather tunics from Peru, chest ornaments from India, frescoes from Ethiopia, and a tenth-century **Dogon statue** from Mali. The reservation-only **Les Ombres** restaurant on the top (fifth) floor embraces views of the Seine and the Tour Eiffel.

37 quai Branly, 7th arr. • www.quaibranly.fr • 01 56 61 70 00
• €€ • Closed Mon. • Métro: Bir-Hakeim

Tour Eiffel

③ French engineer Gustave Eiffel built his lofty, cast-iron structure for the 1889 Universal Exhibition on the centenary of the French Revolution. Constructed from more than 18,000 pieces of iron held together with 2.5 million rivets, it was due to be taken down after 20 years. The advent of radio transmission saved it in the early 20th century, as it provided an ideal location for radio antennae. More than 120 years after it was built, the 1,063-foot-high (324 m) tower has become one of the world's most recognized structures. The tower has **three viewing platforms:** You can reach the first two by stairways—there are more than 300 steps to each level—or elevator. Once there, you'll find restaurants—including the Michelin-starred **Jules Verne** restaurant (01 45 55 61 44, €€€€–€€€€€) on the second level—and panoramic views over Paris. The top platform is reached by elevator only. From here, you can see for 40 miles (64 km) on a clear day, although in bad weather, you may not even be able to see the ground. At night the Eiffel shines like a beacon, and for five minutes each hour on the hour 20,000 lights mounted on the tower sparkle like twinkling stars.

An elevator rises through the Tour Eiffel's intricate network of iron girders. It takes about eight minutes to make a round-trip to the second platform and back.

Parc du Champ de Mars, 5 ave. Anatole, 7th arr. • www.tour-eiffel.com
• 08 92 70 12 39 • To second floor and top: €€, €€€; for stairs: €
• Métro: Bir-Hakeim or École Militaire

Champp de Mars

(4) After the École Militaire (Military Academy) was built in the mid-18th century, the land between it and the Seine was named the Champ de Mars and used for military parades and maneuvers. Now, the lovely green space lined with elm trees and benches is used for festivals and special events, such as Bastille Day fireworks displays (see p. 109), and by picnickers and walkers relishing the gardens and views.

Between ave. de la Bourdonnais and ave. de Suffren, 7th arr. • Métro: Bir-Hakeim or École Militaire

GOOD **EATS**

■ **LE CAMPANELLA**
This typical French brasserie near the École Militaire has been around for decades. It has friendly waiters and reasonably priced food. **18 ave. Bosquet, 7th arr., 01 45 55 73 15, €€**

■ **LES COCOTTES**
Try a salad, an omelette, or a signature meat or fish casserole in a diner setting near the Tour Eiffel. **35 rue St.-Dominique, 7th arr., 01 45 50 10 31, €€**

■ **LA FONTAINE DE MARS**
Classics like *steak frites,* duck confit, and chicken with morels are on the menu at this bistro close to the Tour Eiffel. **129 rue St.-Dominique, 7th arr., 01 47 05 46 44, €€€**

École Militaire

(5) King Louis XV started the Military Academy in 1751. An outstanding example of French classical architecture, its central section, with eight Corinthian columns and a quadrangular dome, was constructed in 1773. In 1785, Napoleon Bonaparte trained here and graduated as a second lieutenant. During the Second Empire, the addition of two wings made for a sprawling complex. From Place de Fontenoy, you can see the Cour d'Honneur flanked by porticoes with twinned columns. The buildings now house military training facilities.

Ave. de la Motte Piquet, 7th arr. • 01 44 42 56 05 • No visits inside the building • Métro: École Militaire

UNESCO

(6) In a true international meeting of minds, a group of three architects—from France, Italy, and the United States—designed the UNESCO Headquarters building. Opened in November 1958, the main building's layout is based on a Y, or three-pointed star. Sculptor Isamu Noguchi created the **Peace Garden,** donated by

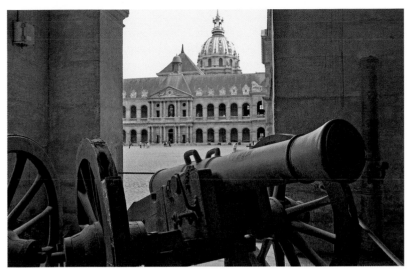
The golden dome of the Église du Dôme rises above the main courtyard of Les Invalides.

the Japanese government. Paths meander past dwarf trees, stands of bamboo, flower beds, and ponds all designed to resemble Japan's natural landscape. Wandering through the grounds, you come across large works of art, such as **"The Fall of Icarus"** by Pablo Picasso, painted on wood panels mounted on a large wall. The Russian Federation gifted Zurab Tseretell's egg-shaped sculpture **"The Birth of a New Man"** to commemorate the 500th anniversary of Christopher Columbus's discovery of America.

7 place de Fontenoy, 7th arr. • www.unesco.org • 01 45 68 10 00 • Closed Sat. and Sun.
• Guided tours available when there is no council meeting • Métro: Ségur or Cambronne

Les Invalides and Musée de l'Armée

7 In 1670, King Louis XIV founded the Hôtel des Invalides as a hospital and home for invalid soldiers, and commissioned the gold-domed chapel, the **Église du Dôme,** for the use of the royal family. Completed in 1706, the chapel is a masterpiece of French classical architecture and houses **Napoleon's tomb.** Napoleon's ashes were brought from St. Helena in 1840, and in 1861 they were placed in six nested coffins inside a massive red quartzite encasement, which stands on a pedestal of dark green granite. Twelve giant figures, representing Napoleon's military victories, surround the tomb. Les Invalides once housed 7,000 veterans. Far fewer live there now, and most of the rooms are given over to a group of military museums. In the Musée de l'Armée, which traces the history of armies from medieval times to today, look for medieval armor and artillery models. The **Musée de l'Ordre de la Libération** has displays devoted to the work of the Resistance from 1940 to 1944. The **Musée des Plan-Reliefs** shows relief maps and model fortresses.

129 rue de Grenelle, 7th arr. • 08 10 11 33 99 or 01 44 42 38 77 • One ticket provides access to the Église du Dôme, the Musée de l'Armée, the Musée des Plans-Reliefs, and the Musée de l'Ordre de la Libération: €€ • Métro: Latour Maubourg or Varenne

SAVVY **TRAVELER**

Between Les Invalides and the Tour Eiffel, pedestrian-friendly **rue Cler** teems with fresh fruit, vegetables, fish, meat, and cheese markets, and tempting patisseries. Behind UNESCO, the **avenue de Saxe** market *(Thurs., Sat.)* brims with vendors selling clothing, jewelry, leather bags, farm-fresh produce, meat, and fish. Listen out for the men bursting into song while throwing their fish back and forth—all in good fun.

Musée Rodin

8 The naturalism, flowing lines, and emotion of Auguste Rodin's sculptures have shocked and delighted audiences in equal measure, and many of these great works now fill the rooms and grounds of the 18th-century Hôtel Biron. At the turn of the 20th century, this rococo-style château provided a temporary residence and workplace for artists Henri Matisse and Jean Cocteau, dancer Isadora Duncan, and Rodin himself. The building now houses works from all stages of his career, plaster models of many of his best-known sculptures, and a display on the bronze casting process. Highlights include one of his first major works, "**The Bronze Age**," a figure of a youth that is so lifelike it scandalized the public of the day, a version of **"The Kiss,"** and the unfinished **"Thought."** One room is dedicated to sculptor Camille Claudel, his onetime companion. Wandering the tranquil, flower-filled garden, you can find several of Rodin's monumental sculptures. **"The Gates of Hell"** is an unfinished bronze door decorated with scenes from Dante's *Inferno*. A small-scale, early version of "The Thinker" appears above the door panels. Nearby, you can see a full-size version of **"The Thinker,"** which Rodin originally entitled "The Poet" because it represents Dante. Also in this part of the garden, **"The Burghers of Calais"** commemorates the six burghers who surrendered the keys of the city of Calais to King Edward III of England in 1347, after a year-long siege. This group memorial captures a range of emotions from despair to defiance.

79 rue de Varenne, 7th arr. • www.musee-rodin.fr • 01 44 18 61 10 • €€, garden only: € • Closed Mon., Jan. 1, May 1, and Dec. 25 • Métro: Varenne or Invalides

Rodin's "Eve" in the 18th-century setting of the Musée Rodin

Musée d'Orsay

*The museum is famous for its unparalleled
collection of Impressionist paintings.*

The main hall of the former railway station is now a light-filled sculpture gallery.

The Musée d'Orsay features European painting, sculpture, drawing,
decorative arts, and photography made between 1848 and 1914. Formed in
the 1980s from the holdings of other major French museums, the collection is
a greatest-hits feast of Édouard Manet, Claude Monet, Paul Cézanne, Vincent
van Gogh, and other superstars alongside equally magnificent works by their
lesser-known contemporaries. The museum also has a fascinating design
collection and temporary exhibitions.

TOUR EIFFEL & LES INVALIDES

■ THE NAVE

The 128-foot-high (39 m) main hall of the former railway station with its arched vault provides a perfect setting for the museum's sculpture collection. Don't miss Jean-Baptiste Carpeaux's **"Dance,"** which caused a scandal when it was first shown, Edgar Degas's **"Small Dancer, Aged 14,"** and Auguste Rodin's **"Balzac."**

■ SNAPSHOTS OF MODERN LIFE

The newly refurbished rooms on Level 3 display work by the Impressionists. While Edgar Degas is best known for his pictures of ballerinas (plenty of which can be found here), his **"In a Café"** (aka "The Absinthe Drinker") provides a realistic and haunting picture of Parisian bars at the end of the 19th century.

The happier side of bourgeois Parisian social life is on display in Pierre-Auguste Renoir's **"Dance at Le Moulin de la Galette,"** in which couples clad in a symphony of blues dance outdoors amid glowing lanterns. Another wonderful rendering of the late 19th century's Golden Age is on display in James Tissot's **"Evening"** (1885), an ode to extravagant fin-de-siècle evening gowns.

■ BEGINNINGS OF MODERN ART

The museum is home to one of Édouard Manet's most famous and scandalous works, **"Luncheon on the Grass"** (Level 3). The painting of art students picnicking alongside a naked woman, in a contemporary rather than allegorical setting, has been copied and referenced by Pablo Picasso and dozens of other painters. Among the many works by Claude Monet (Level 3) is **"Rouen Cathedral: Blue and Gold Harmony, Bright Sunlight."**

Some highlights among the Postimpressionists on Level 2 include Cézanne's **"The Card Players"** and **"Apples and Oranges,"** examples of Cezanne's late works, which influenced the cubists. Also look out for Vincent van Gogh's **"The Church at Auvers"** and a version of **"Bedroom in Arles."**

TOUR EIFFEL & LES INVALIDES

1 rue de la Légion d'Honneur, 7th arr. • www.musee-orsay.fr • 01 40 49 48 14 • €€, special exhibitions: €€ • Closed Mon. • Métro: Solférino

Impressionists in the City

At their first exhibition in Paris in 1874, the Impressionists caused outrage. Claude Monet, Auguste Renoir, Camille Pissarro, Alfred Sisley, and their friends had torn up centuries of tradition that aimed to reproduce the visual world in intricate, accurate detail. Instead they painted quickly and freely, using dabs of vivid color. Their aim was to capture the moment, to paint a spontaneous response to the reality that they saw around them. And one of their prime subjects was Paris.

Auguste Renoir (above) at work out of doors around 1910; his "Dance at Le Moulin de la Galette" (right)

Modern Life

Impressionists rejected the historical and allegorical subject matter of the time, wanting to paint their own world: bourgeois, metropolitan, pleasurable. Paris was still undergoing Baron Haussmann's massive replanning (see p. 8–9), opening up grand boulevards and putting in gas lighting, tramlines, piped water, and sewers. The Impressionists caught the energy of a city on the move.

In Search of Subject Matter

The Impressionists liked to work outdoors. In 1869, Monet and Renoir went to a popular bathing place called La Grenouillère at Croissy-sur-Seine, west of Paris, to depict Parisians at play, boating and bathing; it also proved the perfect location for testing their painting technique on the flickering effects of light on water. Monet was also attracted to industrial scenes and in 1876 and 1877 made a series of studies at the Gare St.-Lazare, recording the steam, energy, and activity of a busy Paris railway station. Renoir was drawn to restaurants and the outdoor dance-café at the Moulin de la Galette in Montmartre. Pissarro painted the city's busy streets and bridges filled with horse-drawn traffic. Sisley painted barges on the Seine.

The Path to Fame

Within 20 years Impressionism had been accepted, and other artists took the experiment in different directions. Henri de Toulouse-Lautrec brought a new, more decadent vision to the dance halls and bars of Paris, while Georges Seurat applied his pointillist technique to Parisian subjects. For the power to communicate contemporary Parisian life across the centuries, nothing quite matches the work of the Impressionists during the 1870s.

IMPRESSIONIST TECHNIQUE

Several of the Impressionists worked out of doors in order to study the changing effects of light and weather. They tried out new types of composition, painting subjects from unusual angles or cropping parts out. To create luminosity across the whole canvas, they applied the paint in individual strokes and dabs of color, rather than mixing colors on the palette and blending brushstrokes together. And they suggested figures and forms rather than painting them in detail.

Cafés & Brasseries

A good reason to go to Paris is to sit in a café and let the hours drift by as you sip coffee and write your next novel, or people-watch, or daydream. Or relax over a beer or glass of wine in a brasserie; these small restaurants traditionally have beer on tap and serve single dishes or larger meals all day.

■ PEOPLE-WATCHING CAFÉS
Café Constant (*139 rue St.-Dominique, 7th arr., 01 47 53 73 34*), close to Les Invalides, serves above-par food for a local café thanks to its award-winning chef. Named for the exquisite horseshoe-shape zinc bar that dominates the room, **Le Petit Fer à Cheval** (*30 rue Vieille du Temple, 4th arr., 01 42 72 47 47*) is a great place for *un verre* and watching the cast of Marais characters wandering in and out.

In the non-touristy part of Montmartre, **Le Sancerre** (*35 rue des Abbesses, 18th arr., 01 42 58 08 20*) is the bar/café for watching the neighborhood locals and the Montmartre artists and hipsters. Open daily, it gets crowded at lunch and in the late evening.

Chez Prune (*36 rue Beaurepaire, 10th arr., 01 42 41 30 47*) is the bohemian bistro that helped turn the Canal St.-Martin area hip. The *steak*

frites are among the city's best, as is the people-watching, which comes with a view of the canal.

■ ICONIC CAFÉS
The chic **Café de Flore** (*172 blvd. St.-Germain, 6th arr., 01 45 48 55 26*) has been a fixture on the busy boulevard St.-Germain since it opened in the late 1800s, and the café's ambience and art deco interior haven't changed much over the years. Located around the corner is the more famous **Les Deux Magots** (*6 place St.-Germain-des-Prés, 6th arr., 01 45 48 55 25*). These two cafés, frequented by the intellectuals of the 1950s and '60s, including Jean-Paul Sartre and Simone de Beauvoir, are well known and expensive.

■ HISTORIC CAFÉS
Order a coffee or a glass of champagne at **Café de la Paix** (*5 place de l'Opéra, 9th arr., 01 40 07 36 36*) and linger at

Historic **Café de Flore** is still a popular place to meet friends and relax.

this beautiful terrace café. Both the café and its regal neighbor, the Opéra Garnier, were designed by architect Charles Garnier. The waiters can be brusque, but the place is steeped in history and dripping with glamour. **Lipp** *(151 blvd. St.-Germain, 6th arr., 01 45 48 53 91)* is more than a brasserie—it's a piece of Paris history. In the mid-20th century, Lipp drew influential people, just like its St.-Germain near-neighbors Flore and Les Deux Magots. You might still glimpse a senator or a celebrity lunching or drinking at Lipp, which began in 1880 as a brasserie offering beer and choucroute.

■ Classic Brasseries

The muses of the four seasons—a classic art nouveau motif—decorate the walls of **Julien** *(16 rue du Faubourg St.-Denis, 10th arr., 01 42 47 00 65)*. The service is thoughtful and attentive, and for dessert the hot Valrhona chocolate sauce served with a flourish on profiteroles is dreamy. Situated at the tip of Île St.-Louis, the classic **Brasserie de l'Île St.-Louis** *(55 quai de Bourbon, 4th arr., 01 43 54 02 59)* from 1870 is still family-owned, with cold beer on tap year-round and mulled wine *(vin chaud)* in winter. The terrace has views of the back of Notre-Dame.

Montmartre

Perched on a hilltop known as La Butte, Montmartre in northern Paris has always stood apart from the rest of the city. Yet it captures the essence of Old Paris like no other neighborhood. Its signature landmark is the magnificent Basilique du Sacré-Coeur—a great starting point for any first-time visitor—but it's in the winding streets that slope down from the basilica that this hilltop enclave shows its real character. The cobblestone roads with their romantic street lamps evoke a sense of the late 19th century, when artists flocked to this once tiny village that became synonymous with high bohemian living. Follow in the footsteps of its famous residents at the Place du Tertre, where Pablo Picasso once painted, and the Moulin de la Galette, the windmill immortalized by painter Pierre-Auguste Renoir, and as you stroll along the gorgeous avenue Junot. Of course, Montmartre can be a tourist trap, but take time out among its squares and hills and you'll still feel its bohemian pulse.

◀ Montmartre's atmospheric streets have been the setting for films such as *Moulin Rouge!* and *La Vie en Rose.*

Montmartre

On this walk through Montmartre's old streets, from the Basilique du Sacré-Coeur to the Moulin de la Galette, you'll get a real taste of the area's village feel.

❶ Basilique du Sacré-Coeur (see pp. 168–169) Climb up into the dome of this famous Parisian landmark for breathtaking views of the city. Outside, head west to rue Azais, then turn right onto rue du Mont Cenis.

❷ St.-Pierre de Montmartre (see p. 164) Discover one of Paris's oldest churches, built on the site of an ancient Roman temple. Outside, head west on rue Norvins, then turn left.

❸ Place du Tertre (see pp. 164–165) This pretty square, with its street artists and colorful cafés, is a great place to people-watch. Head north on rue du Mont Cenis, and turn left onto rue Cortot.

7 Musée Gustave Moreau (see p. 167) This museum, adapted from Gustave Moreau's family home, houses more than 7,000 works of art by the symbolist artist.

```
0 ———————— 600 meters
0 ———————— 600 yards
```

6 Moulin de la Galette (see p. 166) Montmartre's two remaining windmills were immortalized by painters Pierre-Auguste Renoir and Vincent van Gogh. Head west on rue Lepic, turn left at boulevard de Clichy, right down rue de Pigalle and onto rue de La Rochefoucauld.

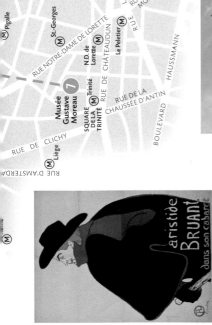

4 Musée de Montmartre (see p. 165) Find out all you need to know about the history of Montmartre and the lives of its most famous residents in this quirky little museum. Walk west on rue Cortot, cross rue des Saules, and continue west on rue de Abreuvoir. Turn north on rue Girardon and left onto avenue Junot.

5 Avenue Junot (see p. 166) Soak up the atmosphere of this elegant, leafy street with gracious houses and artists' studios. Turn south on rue Girardon.

MONTMARTRE DISTANCE: APPROX. 1.6 MILES (2.5 KM)
TIME: APPROX. 6–8 HOURS METRO START: ABBESSES OR ANVERS

MONTMARTRE

Basilique du Sacré-Coeur

1 See pp. 168–169.

Parvis du Sacré-Coeur, 18th arr. • www.sacre-coeur-montmartre.com
• 01 53 41 89 00 • Dome and crypt: € • Métro: Abbesses or Anvers (then take the funicular railway from Funiculaire Gare Basse; you can use a standard métro ticket)

St.-Pierre de Montmartre

2 Dwarfed by the great Sacré-Coeur basilica opposite, St.-Pierre has none of the opulence of its grander neighbor, but there's still plenty to see. This simple church is Paris's second oldest (after St.-Germain-des-Prés; see p. 74) and is all that remains of Montmartre's Benedictine abbey, founded by King Louis VI and his wife, Adélaïde de Savoie, its first abbess, in 1133. The last abbess was guillotined during the revolution and the abbey was closed. It was reconsecrated in 1908. There have been many renovations over the years, but original features include the 12th-century **vaulted choir** and four **marble columns** said to have come from a Roman temple that once stood on the site. The northern aisle contains the **tomb of Adélaïde de Savoie**. If you are passing by on November 1, you can visit the tiny adjoining cemetery—the oldest in Paris—which opens on this one day only. It houses the graves of sculptor Jean-Baptiste Pigalle and explorer Louis de Bougainville, who gave his name to the shrub bougainvillea.

2 rue du Mont Cenis, 18th arr. • 01 46 06 57 63 • Métro: Abbesses or Anvers (then take the funicular railway from Funiculaire Gare Basse)

St.-Pierre de Montmartre's modern stained-glass windows date from 1953.

Place du Tertre

3 Montmarte's pretty tree-lined square is the historic heart of bohemian Paris, where artists including Claude Monet, Pierre-Auguste Renoir, and Pablo Picasso once painted. Today, it's full of street artists, expensive cafés, and tourists, but some of the area's original spirit remains in its old buildings. **À la Mère Catherine** *(No. 6, 01 46 06 32 69, €€€)* is said to be Paris's oldest bistro: Following the 1814 Battle of Paris, Cossack soldiers who ate here would shout *"Bistro!"* (Russian for "Quick!"), inadvertently creating a new kind of Parisian restaurant. The house at **No. 21** was once the home of the Montmartre Free Commune, founded in 1920 to preserve the free-thinking spirit of the area. The commune proposed a number of eccentric policies, including banning December, January, and February, and limiting the number of tourists visiting the area. Ironically, the building now houses the tourist office.

Place du Tertre, 18th arr. • Métro: Abbesses or Anvers (then take the funicular railway from Funiculaire Gare Basse)

Musée de Montmartre

4 This showcase of Montmartre's cultural and historical life is located in a 17th-century house—the oldest in the area. From 1875 onward, it was converted into studios that were used by artists Renoir, Raoul Dufy, Maurice Utrillo, and Suzanne Valadon. Today, the lower floors are devoted to displays about Montmartre's history through France's revolutions and wars, while the upper floors evoke the hedonistic days of the area's artistic life. Highlights include a reconstruction of Utrillo's favorite café, **L'Abreuvoir,** the original painted sign of the famous local cabaret, **Au Lapin Agile,** and artworks by Utrillo, Dufy, and Henri de Toulouse-Lautrec. Also don't miss a reproduction of novelist Roland Dorgelès's hoax painting, **"Sunset over the Adriatic"** (1910), which was acclaimed by the critics until he revealed that he and a group of friends had produced it by attaching a brush to a donkey's tail in a satirical attack on modern art.

12 rue Cortot, 18th arr. • 01 49 25 89 37 • Closed Mon., Jan. 1, and Dec. 25 • €€ • Métro: Anvers (then take the funicular railway from Funiculaire Gare Basse)

GOOD **EATS**

■ **BISTROT POULBOT**
This bistro behind Sacré-Coeur serves classic French food with a twist. **39 rue Lamarck, 18th arr., 01 46 06 86 00, €–€€**

■ **UN ZÈBRE À MONTMARTRE**
A Lyonnais-style restaurant in the Abbesses neighborhood that serves generous portions at good prices. Try the duck confit. **38 rue Lepic, 18th arr., 01 42 23 97 80, €**

MONTMARTRE

Avenue Junot

⑤ A century ago, avenue Junot was part of a scrubby, overgrown area of maquis inhabited by vagrants. Now it is the last word in chic, with an elegance and exclusivity that has earned it the nickname "Champs-Élysées of Montmartre." This broad, tree-lined thoroughfare, home to wealthy Montmartrois, is graced with fabulous private houses and painters' studios. Look in particular for: **No. 13,** the former home of the early 20th-century illustrator Francisque Poulbot, known for his drawings of street urchins (you can see his colorful mosaics of children outside the house); **No.15,** the cubist house of the Romanian poet and founder of dadaism, Tristan Tzara, designed by the architect Adolf Loos; and, at **No. 23 bis,** the Villa Léandre, a group of fairy-tale art deco houses with beautiful gardens.

Ave. Junot, 18th arr. • Métro: Lamarck

Moulin de la Galette

⑥ One of Montmartre's two remaining wooden windmills (there were once 14), the Moulin de la Galette on rue Lepic was built in 1622, when it was known as the Blute-fin. Originally just a humble mill used to press grapes and grind grain, it had a change of fortunes in the 19th century, when the Debray family bought it and used it to make a type of rye bread called *galette.* The bread, served with a glass of milk, became so popular that the mill's name was changed to Moulin de la Galette. Over the years the Debrays replaced the milk with wine, and by the end of the century the mill had become a hugely popular dance hall and the center of Paris's social scene. It was immortalized by artists such as Vincent van Gogh and, most notably, Pierre-Auguste Renoir, whose "Dance at Le Moulin de la Galette" (see pp. 155, 157) now hangs in the Musée d'Orsay (see pp. 154–155). Today the Moulin de la Galette is closed to the public. Nearby on rue Lepic, the **Moulin Radet,** another mill owned by the Debrays, towers above a modern restaurant called **Moulin de la Galette.**

Rue Lepic, 18th arr. • Métro: Lamarck

Moulin Radet, built in 1717 on a nearby site, moved to its current location in 1924.

Musée Gustave Moreau

7 This little-visited museum dedicated to the fantastical works of symbolist painter Gustave Moreau (1825–1898) holds an astonishing legacy of 1,000 of his oil and watercolor paintings, plus 7,000 drawings and a superb collection of his unfinished sketches. The gallery is in the home that Moreau shared with his parents; he designed it himself to display his works in the way he wanted. The collection includes **"Apollo and Pegasus"** and **"The Unicorns."** Both paintings demonstrate the artist's fascination with mythology, which he depicted with vivid swirls of color. You can also see the Moreau family's small apartment rooms, which are crammed with personal belongings and furniture, and Moreau's study and collection of rare books.

14 rue de la Rochefoucauld, 9th arr. • 01 48 74 38 50 • Closed Tues., Jan. 1, May 1, and Dec. 25 • € • Métro: Trinité

Basilique du Sacré-Coeur

Perched on top of Montmartre, the magnificent Basilica of the Sacred Heart was built as a symbol of national reconciliation and hope.

You can avoid the 225 steps up to Sacré-Coeur by taking the funicular railway.

This landmark church, built to symbolize the return of France's self-confidence after its defeat in the 1871 Franco-Prussian war, is dedicated to the Sacred Heart of Jesus. The basilica was built atop the hill because, according to legend, St. Denis—the city's patron saint—was martyred there. Construction began in 1875 with a Romano-Byzantine design by architect Paul Abadie, and it took 39 years to complete. The 272-foot-high (83 m) structure is built from travertine, a form of limestone that bleaches with age, so the church retains its pale color.